Level by Level
Programmes of Study
for
National Curriculum
Mathematics

CW00520589

Level by Level

PoS Mathematics

LEVEL

6

Level by Level
PoS Mathematics
is written by
Marion Teed
and
William Eden
Karen Rose
Eric Martin

Publishing

EHC Publishing
Bradford on Avon • London

INTRODUCTION

The *Level by Level PoS Mathematics* scheme comprises student books structured into Programmes of Study units for Ma1, Ma2, Ma3 and Ma4 for each Level of the (Dearing) National Curriculum. The student books are accompanied by Teacher's Guides. There is a student book and Teacher's Guide for each National Curriculum Level.

This book provides students with classwork for Level 6.

The scheme is supported by *Level by Level Mathematics National Curriculum CHECKERS* (see below). Together, the two schemes provide a complete course of National Curriculum learning material and assessment for each National Curriculum Level.

THE STRUCTURE OF THE PROGRAMMES OF STUDY

The Level Description for each Attainment Target, Ma1, Ma2, Ma3, Ma4, in the (Dearing) National Curriculum is broken down into components LD1, LD2, ... These components are listed at the beginning of each Attainment Target [see page 1 (Ma1), page 9 (Ma2), page 54 (Ma3) and page 84 (Ma4) in this student book]. Each LD component is itself divided into one or more Programmes of Study units (PoS1, PoS2, ...), the number varying according to the mathematical requirement of the component. These Programmes of Study units provide the classroom work for students.

There is a complementary scheme of student books and Teacher's Guides, *Level by Level Mathematics National Curriculum CHECKERS*, which is used by schools for **revision**, **homework** and **assessment**. For each Programmes of Study unit and Level Description component, there are two CHECKERS. The appropriate CHECKERS for each component of work in this student book are listed in the Teacher's Guide.

Published by
EHC Publishing
PO Box 1780
Bradford on Avon
Wilts
BA15 1YD

Tel: 01225 862879
Fax: 01225 863337

Bradford on Avon • London

© EHC Publishing 1995

First Published 1995
Reprinted 1996

All rights reserved. No part of this publication may be reproduced, stored in a retrieval system, or transmitted in any form or by any means, electronic, mechanical, photocopying, recording, or otherwise without either the prior written permission of the Publishers or a licence permitting restricted copying issued by the Copyright Licensing Agency Ltd, 33-34 Alfred Place, London, WC1E 7DP.

Illustrations by Vicki Cohen & Maeve Cook
Printed in Great Britain by Tadberry Evedale Ltd, London

Set in Octavian MT 12 pt

ISBN 1-872936-67-9

CONTENTS

CONTENTS continued

Ma3 Shape, Space and Measures

LD1 Recognise and use common 2-D representations of 3-D objects.

LD2: Know and use the properties of quadrilaterals in classifying different types of quadrilateral.

LD3: Solve problems using angle and symmetry properties of polygons and properties of intersecting and parallel lines, and explain these properties.

LD4: Devise instructions for a computer to generate and transform shapes and paths.

LD5: Understand and use appropriate formulae for finding circumferences and areas of circles, areas of plane rectilinear figures and volumes of cuboids when solving problems.

LD6: Enlarge shapes by a positive whole-number scale factor.

Ma4 Handling Data

LD1 Pupils collect and record continuous data, choosing appropriate equal class intervals over a sensible range to create frequency tables.

LD2 They construct and interpret frequency diagrams.

LD3 They construct pie charts.

LD4 Pupils draw conclusions from scatter diagrams, and have a basic understanding of correlation.

LD5 When dealing with a combination of two experiments, pupils identify all the outcomes, using diagrammatic, tabular or other forms of communication.

LD6 In solving problems, they use their knowledge that the total probability of all the mutually exclusive outcomes of an experiment is 1.

Ma1
Using and Applying Mathematics

LD1: Pupils carry through substantial tasks and solve quite complex problems by breaking them down into smaller, more manageable tasks.
LD2: They interpret, discuss and synthesise information presented in a variety of mathematical forms.
LD3: Pupils' writing explains and informs their use of diagrams.
LD4: Pupils are beginning to give a mathematical justification for their generalisations; they test them by checking particular cases.

LD1, PoS1: SOLVING PROBLEMS

1   Agnes is solving the Bicycle Problem. ▶
    She thinks: First I need to find the circumference
    of the wheel, in ft. Then I need to divide 5280
    by the result, because 1 mile is 5280 ft.
    This will give me the number of revolutions.
    I will use calculator accuracy for my calculations,
    then round down to a whole revolution at the end.

> **Bicycle Problem**
> The wheels of a bicycle have a diameter of 26 inches. How many full revolutions does each wheel make in a 1 mile journey?
> (Circumference of a circle $= \pi \times$ diameter. Use $\pi = 3.142$)

a) Find the circumference of the wheel in inches.
b) Change your result in part a) to ft.
   (1 ft = 12 inches.)
c) Use your result in part b) to calculate the
   number of revolutions.
   Round the result down to a whole number
   of revolutions.

When you are solving problems, try to make
a plan like Agnes's before you begin.

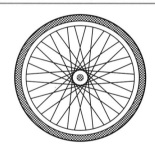

2   a) Look at the Cinema Film Problem.
       Read the plan for solving the problem.
       Write down what is missing from each
       part of the plan.
       [Don't do any calculations until part b).]
       (i)   …… frames are run each second.
             Find how many mm this is.
       (ii) Change the result in (i) to ……
       (iii) Find how many metres of film
             are run each ……
       (iv) Multiply the result in (iii) by
             …… to find the number of
             metres of film for Shane.
    b) Use the plan to solve the problem.

25 mm

> **Cinema Film Problem**
> Cinema films are usually shown on 35 mm film stock. The film is projected at 24 frames per second. The distance from the bottom of one frame to the bottom of the next is 25 mm. The film *Shane* has a running time of 118 minutes. Roughly, how many metres long is the film?

3   Estimate how many minutes of mathematics lessons you will have this term.
    First write down a simple plan which shows the steps to take.

1

4   The drawing shows a half of a cylinder.
    The blue face is a 10 cm square.
    The area of a circle of radius r cm is πr^2 cm^2.
    a) Write down a simple plan showing the
        steps to take in calculating the total surface
        area of the shape correct to the nearest 1 cm^2.
    b) Use your plan to find the total surface
        area of the shape correct to the nearest 1 cm^2.

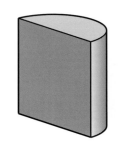

5   Jason is a nature reserve warden on an island.
    He works every day of the week.
    Starting at midnight one Monday, he works 6 hours on,
    6 hours off, 6 hours on, etc.
    Between 8 am and 4 pm wardens are paid £4 per hour.
    Between 4 pm and midnight they are paid £6 per hour.
    Between midnight and 8 am they are paid £8 per hour.
    How much does Jason earn each day?

6   Anna is paving a part of her garden, using
    large square paving slabs.
    The diagram shows the area she is paving.
    The slabs will be laid onto sand 6 cm deep.
    The sand is delivered in bags containing
    0.25 m^3 of sand.
    How many bags should she order?

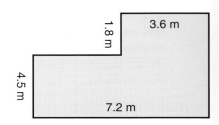

7   The Walker family is planning a canal boat holiday.
    The boat travels at about 3 km per hour and starts
    from the marina in their home town.
    The holiday will be for 7 days and they plan to be
    on the boat, travelling, for about 5 hours each day.
    The boat travels about 4 km on each litre of fuel,
    and the fuel cost is about £1.40 per litre.
    Estimate the total fuel cost for the holiday.

8   The England football team is playing Germany at Wembley.
    The game is hard fought, and end to end throughout.
    The game ends in a 2-2 draw.
    Estimate how far each linesman/lineswoman runs during the game.

9   Choose any wooden table at home or at school.
    Estimate the volume of wood used to make it.

1   Carol asks 150 people how many CDs they own.
    She draws a frequency diagram for the results.
    The median number of CDs is in the class
    interval 10 - 19.
    Which do you think is more likely, A or B ?
    A: The median is 12, correct to 2 SF.
    B: The median is 17, correct to 2 SF.
    Explain your answer.

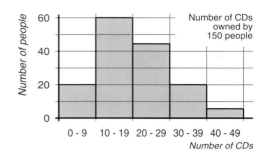

2   The frequency diagram shows the number
    of cups of tea and coffee drunk by people
    in John Fisher's factory yesterday.
    a) The median number of cups of tea is 2.
        What is the median number of cups of
        coffee? Explain your answer.
    b) The mean number of cups of tea is 1.8.
        Is this larger than, less than or equal to
        the mean for cups of coffee?
        Explain your answer.

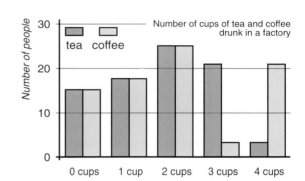

3   Look at the two diagrams.
    They show the ages of people in two villages.
    a) Which village has the greater percentage of
        under-25 year olds? Explain your answer.
    b) Brushwood has a population of 2015.
        Which village has the larger number of
        under-25 year olds? Explain your answer.

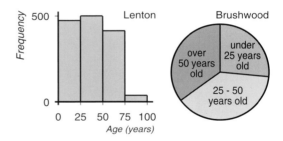

4   Brenda asks 20 people whether they
    • travelled by bus yesterday, or
    • travelled by train yesterday.
    She draws the Venn diagram to show
    her results.
    a) The diagram shows that 11 people
        (8 + 3 people) travelled by bus.
        How many travelled by train?
    b) The diagram shows that 3 people
        travelled by bus *and* by train.
        How many travelled by bus but
        not by train?
    c) How many people did not travel
        by bus or by train?

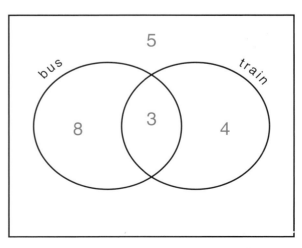

3

5 Rajesh asks 10 people whether they
   travelled by car or by bike yesterday.
   The table shows his results.
   Draw a Venn diagram for the results.

	1	2	3	4	5	6	7	8	9	10
car	✓	✓	✗	✓	✗	✗	✓	✓	✗	✓
bike	✗	✗	✓	✓	✗	✗	✗	✓	✓	✗

6 The diagram shows the Blue Bus Company's
   bus routes between towns A, B, C and D.
   For example, there are two direct routes
   between town A and town D.
   a) Table X shows the same information.
      Copy and complete it.
   b) The Yellow Bus Company also runs
      buses between towns A, B, C and D.
      Table Y gives the number of routes
      between each pair of towns.
      Draw a diagram to show the routes.
   c) The Yellow bus Company has its
      depot in one of the four towns.
      Which town do you think it is? Why?

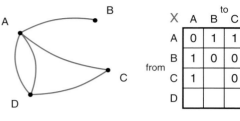

X   to
from \\ X	A	B	C	D
A	0	1	1	2
B	1	0	0	0
C	1		0	
D				0

Y   to
from \\ Y	A	B	C	D
A	0	1	0	0
B	1	0	1	2
C	0	1	0	0
D	0	2	0	0

7 The diagram represents 4 people
   who all send each other a postcard.
   The chart gives the same information.
   a) Draw a diagram, and make out
      a chart, for 5 people who all send
      each other a postcard.
   b) Use the diagrams and the charts
      to help you.
      How many postcards are there
      altogether for 10 people, if they
      all send each other a card?

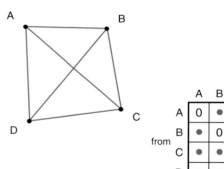

to
from	A	B	C	D
A	0	●	●	●
B	●	0	●	●
C	●	●	0	●
D	●	●	●	0

8 Here is some information about a shape:
   ABCD is a quadrilateral.
   AD = BC; ∠ADC = ∠BCD and
   ∠BAD = ∠CBA.
   The sketch gives the same information.
   Notice how short lines (ᔑ, ⫽) are
   used to show which sides are equal
   and which angles are equal.
   a) Make a sketch for this information:
      PQRS is a quadrilateral.
      PQ = QR; PS = RS;
      ∠SPQ = ∠SRQ.
   b) Write information which agrees
      with the sketch of VWXYZ.

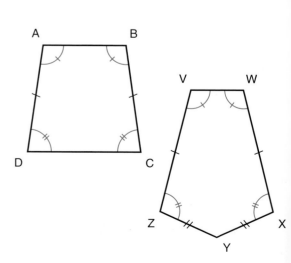

1   Look at the diagram.
    Pam uses it to show that $\frac{1}{3}$ of $\frac{2}{5}$ is $\frac{2}{15}$.
    She says: The blue part is $\frac{2}{5}$ of the rectangle.
              The shaded part is $\frac{1}{3}$ of the blue part;
              but it is also $\frac{2}{15}$ of the rectangle.
              So $\frac{1}{3}$ of $\frac{2}{5}$ is $\frac{2}{15}$.
    a) Draw a diagram to show that $\frac{1}{4}$ of $\frac{3}{7}$ is $\frac{3}{28}$.
       Explain how your diagram works.

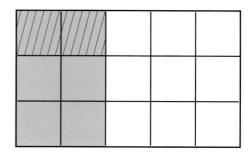

2   Winston carries out a survey to decide which
    sport, football, hockey or athletics, is liked
    best by students in his year group.
    The pie chart shows his results.
    He writes:
    About 57 % of people in my year group
    prefer athletics. Preferences for hockey
    and football are about equal (hockey, 20 %;
    football, 23 %).
    Carla carries out the same survey for her
    year group.
    The pie chart shows her results.
    Write a paragraph like Winston's to explain
    what it shows.

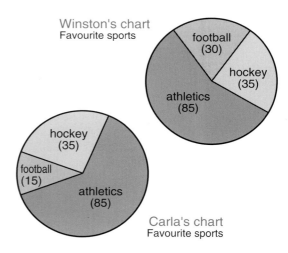

Winston's chart
Favourite sports
football (30)
hockey (35)
athletics (85)

hockey (35)
football (15)
athletics (85)
Carla's chart
Favourite sports

3   Samir draws the diagram to show how the
    heights of four people in his class compare.
    He writes:
    In my diagram, an arrow → means
    'is taller than'.
    So the arrow from A to B means that
    Angie is taller than Ben.
    My diagram shows that Carmen must
    be shortest.
    a) Choose four people in your class.
       Draw a diagram to show how their
       ages compare.
    b) Explain what your diagram shows.

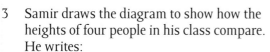

Angie
Ben
Carmen
Dan

4   The diagram is often used to explain that
    the area of a parallelogram can be found
    by multiplying its base length by its height.
    Explain how it does this. (Look for a rectangle
    and a parallelogram with the same area.)

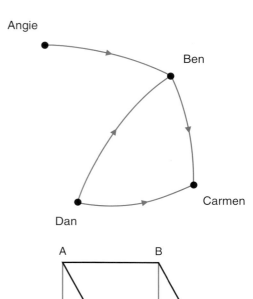

A   B
F   D   E   C

5

5   Jenny makes a list of shoe sizes of students
     in her class, and their heights.
     She draws the scatter diagram to represent
     the information. ▶

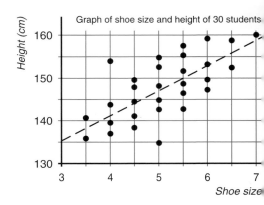
Graph of shoe size and height of 30 students

     She writes:
     My scatter diagram shows that taller
     people in my class tend to have longer
     feet. The broken line suggests how height
     and shoe sizes generally compare.
     There are some important exceptions.
     For example, one student ......

     a) Write down how Jenny might complete
        her last sentence.
     b) The second scatter diagram shows the
        heights and waist measurements of
        people in Jenny's class.
        Write an explanation like Jenny's to
        explain generally what it shows.

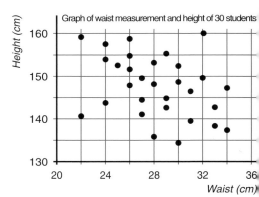
Graph of waist measurement and height of 30 students

     c) Collect information from people in your
        own class about shoe size and arm length
        (tip of fingers to shoulder).
        Draw a scatter diagram.
        Write a short report to explain what your
        diagram shows.

6   Lauren is trying to do this multiplication:
     23×14.
     She says the result can be found by multiplying
     some smaller numbers then adding.
     She writes: 23 is $(20 + 3)$; 14 is $(10 + 4)$.
               So 23×14 is $(20 \times 10) + (3 \times 4)$,
               which is $200 + 12$, which is 212.

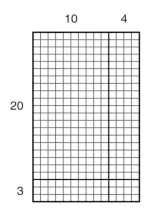

     a) Make a sketch of the diagram.
        Use it to explain why Lauren is wrong.
     b) Use the diagram to explain which numbers
        should be multiplied and added to give
        the correct result.

7   The diagram gives information about the hours
     of sunshine in two towns last June.

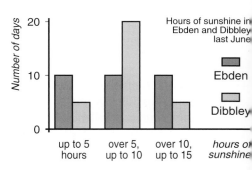
Hours of sunshine in Ebden and Dibbley last June
Ebden
Dibbley

     a) Pam says that the two resorts had the same
        amount of sunshine altogether, because the
        grey columns and the white columns have
        the same total height.
        Explain why she is wrong.
     b) Write a short paragraph to explain how the
        hours of sunshine compare.

1   Pam draws some blue dots and some black dots.
    She draws a line from every blue dot to every
    black dot.
    She says: The total number of lines is equal
    to the number of blue dots times the number
    of black dots.
    a) Show that Pam's rule is true for 2 blue dots
       and 5 black dots.
    b) Use a diagram to help you to explain why
       Pam's rule is true.

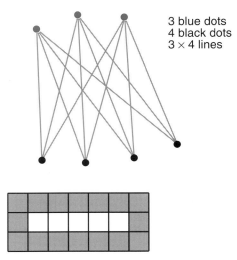

3 blue dots
4 black dots
3 × 4 lines

2   Pavel draws a line of 1 cm squares.
    He surrounds it with a layer of grey 1 cm squares.
    He says: The number of grey squares equals
    twice the number of white squares, plus 6.
    a) Show that Pavel's rule works for a line of
       7 white squares.
    b) Explain why Pavel's rule always works.
    c) Julie surrounds a row of white squares
       with a double layer of blue squares.
       Find a rule for calculating the number of
       blue squares when you know the number
       of white squares.

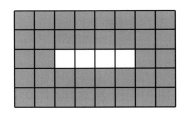

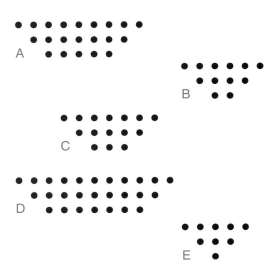

3   The dot patterns belong to the same family.
    a) Avril says: To calculate the total
       number of dots in a pattern, multiply
       the number of dots in the bottom row
       by 3 then add 6.
       Show that her rule works for pattern A.
    b) Use a diagram to help you to explain why
       Avril's rule always works.
    c) Dougal says: To calculate the total
       number of dots in a pattern, add 2 to
       the number of dots in the bottom row
       then multiply by 3.
       Show that his rule works for pattern A.
    d) Use a diagram to help you to explain why
       Dougal's rule always works.

4   These are consecutive whole numbers: ▶   7, 8, 9, 10, 11
    a) Sunita says: When you add 3 consecutive
       whole numbers, the result is a multiple of 3.
       Show that Sunita's rule is true for 6, 7, 8.
    b) Explain why Sunita's rule is always true.

7

5 a) Ross says: When you add 4 consecutive whole numbers, the result
       is always a multiple of 4.
       Give an example to show that he is wrong.
   b) Write a rule that is true for the sum of 4 consecutive whole numbers.

6 a) Write a rule that is true for the sum of 5 consecutive whole numbers.
   b) Show that your rule is true for 12, 13, 14, 15, 16.

7 Jo thinks of a number.
   She adds 1, multiplies the result by 2, subtracts 2, then divides by 2.
   For example: $7 \rightarrow 8 \rightarrow 16 \rightarrow 14 \rightarrow 7$.
   She says: The result is always the number I started with.
   a) Show that Jo's rule is true for the number 10.
   b) This chain shows why the rule is always true:
           $n \rightarrow n+1 \rightarrow 2(n+1) = 2n+2 \rightarrow 2n+2-2 = \ldots\ldots \rightarrow \ldots\ldots$
       Copy and complete it.
   c) Mike thinks of a number.
       He adds 1, multiplies the result by 2, subtracts 4, then divides by 2.
       For example: $7 \rightarrow 8 \rightarrow 16 \rightarrow 12 \rightarrow 6$.
       He says: The result is always 1 less than the number I started with.
       Show that Mike's rule is true for the number 10.
   d) Draw a chain like that in b) which shows why the rule is always true.

8 The dot patterns belong to the same family.
   This is a rule for calculating the number of
   dots in a pattern:
   Count how many dots high the pattern is.
   Multiply this by 1 more than the number
   of dots high it is.
   Divide by 2.
   a) Show that the rule works for pattern A.
   b) Use a diagram to help you to explain
       why the rule is true for all patterns.

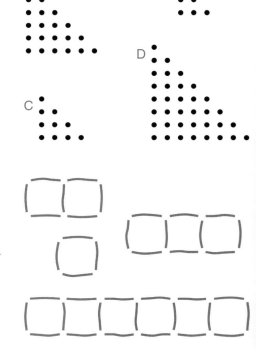

9 The squares patterns are made from sticks.
   a) Check that a pattern with 10 squares is made
       from 31 sticks.
   b) Write down a rule for calculating the number
       of sticks when you know the number of squares.
   c) Show that your rule works for a pattern with
       6 squares.
   d) Write down a rule for finding the number of
       squares when you know the number of sticks.
   e) Show that your rule works for 37 sticks.

Ma2
Number
and Algebra

LD1: Order and approximate decimals when solving numerical problems and equations such as $x^2 = 20$, using trial-and-improvement methods.
LD2: Be aware of which number to consider as 100 per cent, or a whole, in problems involving comparisons, and use this to evaluate one number as a fraction or percentage of another.
LD3: Understand and use the equivalences between fractions, decimals and percentages.
LD4: Calculate using ratios in appropriate situations.
LD5: When exploring number patterns, find and describe in words the rule for the next term or nth term of a sequence where the rule is linear.
LD6: Formulate and solve linear equations with whole number coefficients.
LD7: Represent mappings expressed algebraically, interpreting general features and using graphical representation in four quadrants where appropriate.

LD1, PoS1: ORDERING AND APPROXIMATING DECIMALS

1   Look at the decimal number and the digit headings. ▶
Reading from right to left ←, the headings increase by a factor 10.

| 10000 | ? | 100 | 10 | 1 | $\frac{1}{10}$ | $\frac{1}{100}$ | $\frac{1}{1000}$ | ? |

34856.3052

Write down the heading missing above
a) the digit 4   b) the digit 2.

2   Look at the number.
The decimal point and some of the digits are covered by ink blots.

692   53   427

a) What does the 5 stand for if the 3 stands for
(i) hundreds   (ii) hundredths   (iii) 1000 s   (iv) $\frac{1}{1000}$ s?
b) What does the 3 stand for if the 5 stands for
(i) hundreds   (ii) hundredths   (iii) 1000 s   (iv) $\frac{1}{1000}$ s?
c) What does the 7 stand for if the 4 stands for
(i) 10 000 s   (ii) hundredths   (iii) 1000 s   (iv) $\frac{1}{1000}$ s?

3   Starting with the left hand digit 8, compare the digits in these two numbers. ▶
The first mismatch is the 4th digit from the left.
The number 8.4652 is larger than 8.4639 because it includes 5 thousandths compared with only 3 thousandths.

8.4652
8.4639

Write these numbers with one decimal point beneath the other, then tick ✓ the larger number.
a) 0.032; 0.0032
b) 32.822; 3.2822
c) 24.165 34; 24.166 34
d) 0.200 03; 0.200 001

◀ Example: 34.6702 ✓
               9.418

9

4   Which is smaller,
    a) 0.09 or 0.21   b) 0.002 or 0.0003   c) 0.102 or 0.08   d) 0.005 or 0.014 108 ?

5   Write these numbers in order, smallest first.
    a) 3.01   0.425   0.82   0.5214
    b) 0.246   0.61   0.0098   0.01

6   Write down a number between
    a) 0.34 and 0.82   b) 0.6 and 0.7   c) 0.002 and 0.02   d) 0.0099 and 0.01.

7   Look at the scale. ▶
    It shows that 5.86 is nearer to
    5.9 than 5.8.
    We say that 5.86 is 5.9, correct
    to the nearest 0.1, or **correct
    to 1 decimal place (1 DP)**.

    | 5.8 | | | | | | | | | 5.9 |

    5.86

    a) Is 5.83 nearer to 5.8 or 5.9 ?
    b) Write 5.83 correct to 1 DP.
    c) For 'halfway' numbers we always
       round up: 6.35 correct to 1 DP is 6.4.
       Write these correct to 1 DP:
       (i) 5.55   (ii) 5.95.

8   Write these numbers correct to 1 DP.
    a) 9.68   b) 10.32   c) 0.79   d) 1.67   e) 4.94   f) 0.05
    g) 0.099   h) 0.852   i) 12.08   j) 33.33   k) 17.666   l) 3.982

9   Look at the scale. ▶
    It shows that 5.826 is nearer to
    5.83 than 5.82.
    We say that 5.826 is 5.83, correct
    to the nearest 0.01, or **correct to
    2 decimal places (2 DP)**.

    | 5.82 | | | | | | | | | 5.83 |

    5.826

    a) Is 5.748 nearer to 5.74 or 5.75 ?
    b) Write 5.748 correct to 2 DP.
    c) For 'halfway' numbers we always
       round up: 6.385 correct to 2 DP is 6.39.
       Write these correct to 2 DP:
       (i) 8.735   (ii) 8.955.

10 Write these numbers correct to 2 DP.
    a) 2.638   b) 0.932   c) 0.7239   d) 1.675   e) 4.025   f) 0.0445
    g) 0.039   h) 0.0852   i) 1.008   j) 3.3333   k) 6.6666   l) 6.704

10

11 A runway is 1.3628 km long.
    Write its length correct to
    a) 1 DP   b) 2 DP   c) 3 DP.

12 When we write 6.704 correct to 2 DP, we write 6.70 rather than 6.7.
    a) Why do you think this is?
    b) Write 4.69700249 correct to
        (i) 1 DP   (ii) 2 DP   (iii) 3 DP   (iv) 4 DP   (v) 5 DP   (vi) 6 DP   (vii) 7 DP.

13 Silver wire costs £2.34 for 1 cm.
    How much, correct to 2 DP, does
    a) 8.7 cm of the wire cost
    b) 12 mm of the wire cost
    c) 1 m of the wire cost?

14 Look at the scale. ▶
    It shows that 3.74 is nearer to 3.7
    than 3.8.
    We say that 3.74 is 3.7, **correct
    to 2 significant figures (2 SF)**.

    In 3.74, 3 is the first significant
    figure; ▶
    7 is the second significant figure;
    4 is the third significant figure.

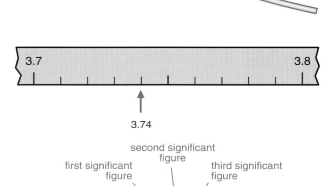

    a) Is 5.82 nearer to 5.8 or 5.9 ?
    b) Write 5.82 correct to 2 SF.
    c) For 'halfway' numbers we
        always round up:
        6.35 correct to 2 SF is 6.4.
        Write these correct to 2 SF:
        (i) 5.15   (ii) 5.95.

15 The first significant figure in any number
    is the first non-zero digit from the left.
    So in 0.0405 the first significant figure is
    the digit 4; the second is the 0 to the right
    of the 4; the third is the 5. ▶

    Write these numbers correct to 2 SF.
    a) 19.38   b) 94.32   c) 0.594   d) 0.606
    e) 456.9   f) 0.0503   g) 0.0991   h) 0.0999
    i) 102.08   j) 330.33   k) 0.666   l) 0.909
    m) 400.9   n) 10.07   o) 6.0091   p) 0.00340
    q) 0.000 811   r) 300.03   s) 0.606 01   t) 0.999

    SF or DP?
    George says that writing
    numbers correct to 2 SF
    and to 1 DP always gives
    the same accuracy.
    Is he correct? Explain
    your answer.
    •••••••••••••••••••••••••••••.

16 Look at the scale. ▶
It shows that 62.48 is nearer
to 62.5 than 62.4.
62.48 is 62.5, **correct to
3 significant figures (3 SF).**

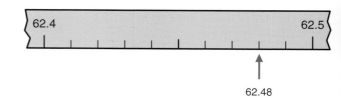

62.4   62.5

↑
62.48

a) Is 128.48 nearer to 128 or 129?
b) Write 128.48 correct to 3 SF.

17 Write 86.3028 correct to
a) 2 SF   b) 1 SF   c) 3 SF   d) 4 SF   e) 5 SF.

18 What is the smallest number which gives
a) 4.6 when written correct to 1 DP?
b) 4.6 when written correct to 2 SF?
c) 0.01 when written correct to 2 DP?
d) 0.010 when written correct to 2 SF?

19 Irene takes a few grains of rice from two bags and weighs them.
She gets 54 grains of pillau rice with a total mass of 8.3 g.
She gets 32 grains of pudding rice with a total mass of 7.3 g.
a) Estimate the mass, in g correct to 2 SF, of a grain of
    (i) pillau rice   (ii) pudding rice.
b) Which type of grain tends to be heavier?

20 Bob lays the grains of rice in Question 19 in straight lines.
The 54 grains of pillau rice have a total length of 44.8 cm.
The 32 grains of pudding rice have a total length of 18.9 cm.
a) Estimate the length, in cm correct to 1 DP, of a grain of
    (i) pillau rice   (ii) pudding rice.
b) Which type of grain tends to be longer?

21 Umesh runs a distance of 50 m in 6.4 seconds.
a) On average, how many m, correct to 1 DP, is this in 1 second?
b) On average, how many seconds, correct to 1 SF, is this for 1 m?
c) Karen runs 30 m in 4.1 seconds.
    Is this slower or faster than Umesh?

22 A bean plant grows 17 mm during a 24 hour period.
a) On average, how many mm is this
    (i) in 1 hour, correct to 1 DP
    (ii) in 1 minute, correct to 2 SF?
b) An ivy grows 69 mm during a 100 hour period.
    Is this slower or faster than the bean plant?

12

1   Barry multiplies a number by itself three times.
    The result is 100.

    ◀ For example, $4.2 \times 4.2 \times 4.2$.

    a) Use your calculator.
       Is the number smaller than 4 or larger than 4?
    b) Is the number smaller than 5 or larger than 5?
    c) Find Barry's number correct to 1 DP.

2   The teacher writes a number on the board.
    Kamlesh adds 5 to it.
    Barry multiplies it by 5.
    They both get the same result.
    a) Which is more nearly correct for the number,
       1.1 or 1.2?
    b) Which is more nearly correct, 1.23 or 1.24?
    c) Find the exact number.

3   Look at the equation.
    Josie is solving it by
    trying different values
    for x.

    $$\frac{94}{x} = 25$$

    She tries $x = 6$: $94 \div 6 = 15.66...$; so $x = 6$ is too big.
    She tries $x = 3$: $94 \div 3 = 31.33...$; so $x = 3$ is too small.
    She tries $x = 4$: $94 \div 4 = 23.5$; so $x = 4$ is too big.

    ◀ The larger x is, the
    smaller is $94 \div x$.

    a) Is the solution of the equation nearer to 3 or to 4?
    b) Which is nearer to the solution, $x = 3.7$ or $x = 3.8$?
    c) Try some values between 3.7 and 3.8.
       Find the exact solution.

4   Josie's method in Question 3 is called **trial and improvement**.

    Pam wants to know what value of k makes $38(k - 3)$ equal to 469.
    a) Try $k = 15.3$. Is this too small or too large?
    b) Try $k = 15.4$. Is this too small or too large?
    c) Which is nearer to the correct solution, 15.3 or 15.4?
    d) Use trial and improvement to find the solution correct to 2 DP.

5   Find the value of n, correct to 1 DP, which makes $\frac{17}{n}$ equal to 93.

6   Use trial and improvement to solve these equations.
    Find each solution correct to 1 DP.

    a) $\frac{21}{x} = 8$ b) $\frac{k}{5.4} = 7.3$ c) $\frac{8}{e} = 17$

7   Efan is solving the equation
    $2d + 34 = 9d + 8$.
    He records his trials in this table. ▶
    Copy the table.
    Record some more trials.
    Find the solution of the equation
    a) correct to 1 DP
    b) correct to 2 DP.

Value of d	Value of $2d + 34$	Value of $9d + 8$	Comment
2	38	26	2 is too small
5	44	53	5 is too big
3	40	35	3 is too small

8   Look at the equation.
    Find the solution correct to 2 DP.
    Record your trials in a table.

$$\frac{h}{8} = \frac{7}{h}$$

9   Ada buys a 150 cm strip of wood to
    make a picture frame.
    She wants the frame to be 20 cm taller
    than it is wide.
    Record your trials in a table like this. ▶
    Find the width of the frame.

width (cm)	height (cm)	perimeter (cm)
5	25	60
10	35	90

10 Two icicles are melting in the sun.
    They both get 1 mm shorter every minute.
    At 8.00 am they are 120 mm and 94 mm long.
    Use trial and improvement.
    Record your results in a table like this. ▶
    At what time is one icicle twice as long
    as the other?

number of minutes	length 1 (mm)	length 2 (mm)
40	80	54
50	70	44

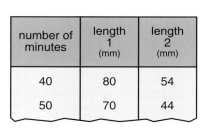

11 A hare and a tortoise have a race.
    The hare runs four times as fast as
    the tortoise, but gives it a 50 m start.
    Use trial and improvement.
    Find how far the hare has run when
    it catches the tortoise, correct to the
    a) nearest m   b) nearest cm.

12 Look at the L shape.
    When d is 10, its area
    is $(5 \times 10) + (8 \times 2)$ cm^2,
    which is 66 cm^2.
    What is the value of d,
    correct to 2 DP, if the
    area of the L shape is
    a) 64 cm^2
    b) 80 cm^2?

12 cm

5 cm

8 cm

d cm

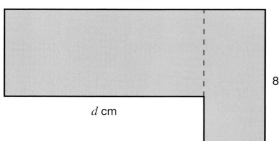

1   Look at rectangle W. ▶

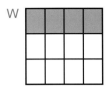
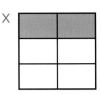

The blue region shows that $\frac{1}{3}$ is the same as $\frac{4}{12}$.

We say that $\frac{1}{3}$ **is equivalent to** $\frac{4}{12}$.

We write $\frac{1}{3} = \frac{4}{12}$.

The blue regions of rectangles X, Y and Z also show fractions equivalent to $\frac{1}{3}$.
Write down the fraction for each one.

2   Sketch a partly shaded rectangle to show that

a) $\frac{1}{4}$ is equivalent to $\frac{2}{8}$ b) $\frac{2}{5}$ is equivalent to $\frac{6}{15}$ c) $\frac{3}{4} = \frac{30}{40}$.

3   Look at the circle.
Write down a pair of equivalent fractions, $\frac{\square}{\square} = \frac{\square}{\square}$, shown by
a) the blue region
b) the white region.

4   Look at shapes A and B.
Write *three* equivalent fractions shown by each blue region.
Write $\frac{\square}{\square} = \frac{\square}{\square} = \frac{\square}{\square}$ for each shape.

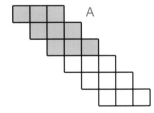
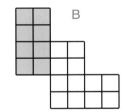

5   Look at the rectangle.
It has been divided into 8 equal pieces.
a) Copy and complete for the fraction shown by the grey region: $\frac{?}{8}$.
b) Pam divides the rectangle into 5 times as many equal pieces.
Copy and complete for the fraction shown by the grey region: $\frac{?}{40}$.
c) Paul divides the rectangle into 80 equal pieces altogether.
What fraction, equivalent to the fractions in part a) and b), is shown by the grey region of his diagram?

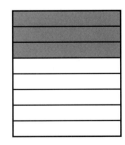

6   Carl divides a rectangle into 7 equal parts.
He shades 4 of them to show the fraction $\frac{4}{7}$.

He now divides the rectangle into 20 times as many equal parts.
What fraction, equivalent to $\frac{4}{7}$, does the shaded region show now?

7   Larry buys some orange squash.
    The instructions say 'Add 4 parts water to 1 part squash'.
    a) What fraction of a glass of orange drink is water?
    b) What fraction of a 2 *l* jug of orange drink is water?
    c) What fraction of 10 glasses of orange drink is water?

8   Think about the fraction $\frac{2}{3}$.
    The 2 is called the **numerator** of the fraction.
    The 3 is called the **denominator**.
    The diagrams show that if we multiply the
    numerator and denominator by the same
    number, we get an equivalent fraction. ▶
    Examples:
    $\frac{2 \times 2}{2 \times 3} = \frac{4}{6}$, $\frac{3 \times 2}{3 \times 3} = \frac{6}{9}$, $\frac{5 \times 2}{5 \times 3} = \frac{10}{15}$.

$\frac{2}{3}$

$\frac{4}{6}$ $\frac{6}{9}$ $\frac{10}{15}$

    a) Multiply the numerator and denominator of each fraction by 3.
        Write down the equivalent fraction this gives.
        A: $\frac{3}{5}$ B: $\frac{2}{7}$ C: $\frac{5}{8}$

    b) Multiply the numerator and denominator of each fraction by 10.
        Write down the equivalent fraction this gives.
        A: $\frac{5}{9}$ B: $\frac{1}{4}$ C: $\frac{6}{7}$

9   Kath is finding fractions equivalent to $\frac{3}{8}$.
    Copy and complete each of these.

    a) $\frac{3}{8} \xrightarrow{\times 4} \frac{12}{?}$ ($\times 4$)
    b) $\frac{3}{8} \xrightarrow{\times 5} \frac{15}{?}$ ($\times ?$)
    c) $\frac{3}{8} \xrightarrow{\times ?} \frac{?}{16}$ ($\times ?$)
    d) $\frac{3}{8} \xrightarrow{\times ?} \frac{18}{?}$ ($\times ?$)
    e) $\frac{3}{8} \xrightarrow{\times ?} \frac{?}{80}$ ($\times ?$)

10 Copy and complete these fraction sentences.

    a) $\frac{4}{5} = \frac{?}{15}$
    b) $\frac{5}{6} = \frac{?}{30}$
    c) $\frac{2}{9} = \frac{16}{?}$
    d) $\frac{1}{2} = \frac{50}{?}$
    e) $\frac{15}{20} = \frac{?}{4}$

11 Think of the fraction $\frac{16}{20}$.
    Dividing has the opposite effect to multiplying.
    So dividing the numerator and denominator
    by the same number will give an equivalent fraction.
    Examples:
    $\frac{16 \div 2}{20 \div 2} = \frac{8}{10}$, $\frac{16 \div 4}{20 \div 4} = \frac{4}{5}$.

    Divide the numerator and denominator of each fraction by 3.
    Write down the equivalent fraction this gives.
    A: $\frac{3}{6}$ B: $\frac{15}{18}$ C: $\frac{18}{36}$

12 Copy and complete.

a) $\frac{8}{12} \xrightarrow{\div 4} \frac{2}{?}$ (top $\div 4$, bottom $\div 4$)   b) $\frac{10}{25} \xrightarrow{\div 5} \frac{2}{?}$ (bottom $\div ?$)   c) $\frac{14}{16} \xrightarrow{\div ?} \frac{?}{8}$ (bottom $\div ?$)   d) $\frac{12}{30} \xrightarrow{\div ?} \frac{2}{?}$ (bottom $\div ?$)   e) $\frac{30}{40} \xrightarrow{\div ?} \frac{?}{8}$ (bottom $\div ?$)

13 Copy and complete these fraction sentences.

a) $\frac{12}{24} = \frac{?}{2}$ b) $\frac{40}{60} = \frac{?}{3}$ c) $\frac{35}{45} = \frac{7}{?}$ d) $\frac{72}{88} = \frac{9}{?}$ e) $\frac{?}{45} = \frac{3}{5}$

14 By dividing the numerator and denominator, we can write $\frac{56}{72}$ as $\frac{28}{36}$, or $\frac{14}{18}$, or $\frac{7}{9}$.
$\frac{7}{9}$ is the equivalent fraction which uses the smallest possible whole numbers.
We say that $\frac{56}{72}$ written in its **lowest terms** is $\frac{7}{9}$.

Write these fractions in their lowest terms.

a) $\frac{20}{80}$ b) $\frac{64}{96}$ c) $\frac{39}{52}$ d) $\frac{77}{91}$ e) $\frac{48}{64}$

15 Look at these two fractions.
a) Write each one with denominator 24.
b) Which fraction is the larger?

$$\frac{3}{8} \qquad \frac{5}{12}$$

16 Kevin wants to know which is larger, $\frac{7}{12}$ or $\frac{11}{16}$.
He writes each fraction with denominator 48.
a) Write down the two equivalent fractions he obtains.
b) Which fraction is larger?

17 Write down the larger of each pair of fractions.

a) $\frac{3}{4}$, $\frac{7}{10}$ b) $\frac{3}{4}$, $\frac{5}{6}$ c) $\frac{7}{18}$, $\frac{4}{9}$ d) $\frac{2}{7}$, $\frac{3}{11}$ e) $\frac{7}{10}$, $\frac{5}{8}$

18 Look at these sets of fractions.
For each set, change the fractions to equivalent fractions with the same denominator.
Circle the largest fraction.

a) $\frac{1}{2}$, $\frac{5}{6}$, $\frac{3}{4}$ b) $\frac{1}{4}$, $\frac{3}{14}$, $\frac{2}{7}$ c) $\frac{1}{3}$, $\frac{3}{7}$, $\frac{2}{5}$ d) $\frac{5}{8}$, $\frac{13}{20}$, $\frac{3}{4}$

19 a) Add 1 to the numerator and the denominator of $\frac{3}{10}$.
      Write down the result.
   b) Is the new fraction an equivalent fraction, a larger fraction, or a smaller fraction? Explain how you decided.

In between
Find a fraction between $\frac{5}{8}$ and $\frac{5}{9}$.

1   Read the satellite TV problem. ▶

To solve it we can compare fractions:

$\frac{8}{20}$ of the houses in Lime Road have satellite TV.

$\frac{10}{30}$ of those in Ripley Road have satellite TV.

To answer the question we compare $\frac{8}{20}$ and $\frac{10}{30}$:

$\frac{8}{20} = \frac{24}{60}$; $\frac{10}{30} = \frac{20}{60}$. So $\frac{8}{20}$ is larger than $\frac{10}{30}$.

So satellite TV is more popular in Lime Road.

Another house in Ripley Road gets satellite TV.
Is satellite TV still more popular in Lime Road?
Explain your answer.

> 8 of the 20 houses in Lime Road have satellite television.
> 10 of the 30 houses in Ripley Road have satellite television.
> In which road is satellite television more popular?

2   a) A survey shows that 8 out of 10 Red Line buses arrive on time.
        What fraction is this?
     b) In the same survey, 5 out of 6 Speedwell buses arrive on time.
        What fraction is this?
     c) Which buses keep better time, Red Line or Speedwell?
         Explain your answer.

3   a) Bruce orders 4 dozen eggs from Sunfresh Farm.
        5 eggs are cracked.
        What fraction is this?
     b) Kirsty orders 6 dozen eggs from Wilson's Farm.
        7 eggs are cracked.
        What fraction is this?
     c) Which farm seems to have fewer cracked eggs?
        Explain your answer.

Goals comparison
Find a newspaper which contains the football results for teams in a UK football league.
Which does your league suggest is most likely:
in drawn games no goals are scored,
or
in away wins one team scores no goals,
or
in home wins one team scores no goals ?
Explain your answer.
●●●●●●●●●●●●●●●●●●●●●●●●●●●

4   There are two displays of bathroom tiles in Carter's shop.
     The Chatsworth display has 40 tiles, 12 of which are patterned.
     The Holyrood display has 60 tiles, 14 of which are patterned.
     Which display has the larger proportion of patterned tiles?
     Explain your answer.

5   a) What fraction of pattern
         A is coloured blue?
     b) What fraction of pattern
         B is coloured blue?
     c) Which pattern has the larger
         proportion of blue?

A 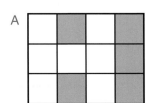   B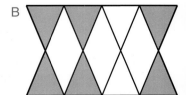

6   a) Which is greater, the fraction of names of days of the
        week which contain the letter 'u', or
        the fraction of names of months of the year that contain
        the letter 'u' ?
        Explain how you decided.
    b) What fraction of 48 kg is equal to two-thirds of 24 kg ?
    c) What fraction of 16 cm is equal to five-twelfths of 24 cm ?

7   Carl's mug holds 265 ml of coffee.
    He has 3 teaspoonfuls of sugar.
    Winston's mug holds 180 ml of coffee.
    He has 2 teaspoonfuls of sugar.
    Whose coffee is sweeter?
    Explain how you decided.

8   Penwick Farm has 70 sheep, 55 cows and 25 pigs.
    Rollings Farm has 44 sheep, 28 cows and 18 pigs.
    a) Copy and complete the table.
    b) Which farm has the greater proportion of
        (i)   sheep
        (ii) cows
        (iii) pigs ?

| | Fraction of all animals on | |
	Penwick Farm	Rollings Farm
sheep	$\frac{7}{15}$	
cows		
pigs		

9   There are 20 houses in Ridgeway Road.
    4 of the front doors are red, and 5 are blue.
    There are 50 houses in Westminton Road.
    7 of the front doors are red, and 12 are blue.
    a) In which Road are red front doors more
        popular? Explain your answer.
    b) In which Road are blue front doors more
        popular? Explain your answer.

10 Thirty students were asked 'Do you play tennis or hockey?'
    The table shows the results.
    a) Write in its lowest terms, the fraction of the students who
        (i)   play hockey only
        (ii) play both tennis and hockey
        (iii) do not play either sport.
    b) Is hockey more popular amongst those who play tennis,
        or those who do not play tennis? Explain your answer.

tennis only	8
hockey only	3
tennis and hockey	6
neither	3

11 The table shows what bread
    Pam ate over the weekend.
    Is she more inclined to toast
    white bread or brown bread?
    Explain your answer.

	brown	white
toasted	2	1
plain	8	3

1   We sometimes need to compare fractions and percentages.
    Example:
    Cliftons say that 64 % of their jam is real fruit.
    Miltons say that three-fifths of their jam is real fruit.
    Which jam has more real fruit per kg?
    Solution:
    64 % is $\frac{64}{100}$.
    Three-fifths $\left(\frac{3}{5}\right)$ is $\frac{20 \times 3}{20 \times 5} = \frac{60}{100}$.
    So Cliftons' jam has more real fruit per kg.

   a) Write $\frac{2}{5}$ as a fraction with denominator 100.
   b) Which is larger, 45 % or $\frac{2}{5}$?

2   a) Write $\frac{13}{20}$ as a fraction with denominator 100.
    b) Which is larger, 60 % or $\frac{13}{20}$?

3   a) Write each fraction with denominator 100.
        A: $\frac{9}{20}$ B: $\frac{3}{4}$ C: $\frac{7}{10}$ D: $\frac{1}{2}$
    b) Which of the fractions are smaller than 55 % ?

4   Write down which is larger, the fraction or the percentage.
    a) 29 %; $\frac{3}{10}$ b) 37 %; $\frac{7}{20}$ c) 79 %; $\frac{4}{5}$

5   72 % of the Bintje potato plants, and $\frac{17}{25}$ of the
    Cara potato plants in a garden get blight.
    a) Write $\frac{17}{25}$ as a fraction with denominator 100.
    b) Which type of potato plant is more resistant
        to blight?

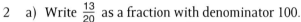
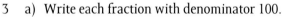
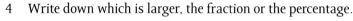
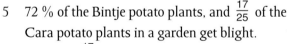

6   a) Write each percentage as a fraction with denominator 100.
        A: 34 %   B: 56 %   C: 68 %   D: 45 %
    b) Write each fraction in part a) in its lowest terms.

7   Write each percentage as a fraction in its lowest terms.
    a) 65 %   b) 72 %   c) 33 %   d) 84 %   e) 24 %   f) 88 %

8   At an athletics match 32 % of the spectators are from Canada, and $\frac{7}{20}$ are from France.
    Are there more Canadian or more French spectators? Explain your answer.

9   We can compare fractions and percentages also by using decimals.
    This is useful when the fraction does not easily convert into one
    with denominator 100.
    Example:
    Which is larger $\frac{26}{40}$ or 63 % ?
    Solution:
    $\frac{26}{40}$ is 26 ÷ 40, which is 0.65.
    63 % is $\frac{63}{100}$, which is 0.63.
    So $\frac{26}{40}$ is larger.

    Use a calculator.
    a) Write these fractions as decimals.

        A: $\frac{17}{20}$ B: $\frac{13}{52}$ C: $\frac{72}{150}$ D: $\frac{24}{60}$ E: $\frac{36}{80}$ F: $\frac{38}{200}$

    b) Which of the fractions in part a) are larger than 42 % ?

10 Write each fraction and percentage as a decimal.
    Underline the larger number.
    a) 43 %; $\frac{12}{25}$ b) 93 %; $\frac{69}{75}$ c) 13 %; $\frac{9}{60}$

11 64.5 % as a decimal is 0.645.   ◀ 64.5 ÷ 100 is 0.645
    Write each of these as decimals:
    a) 34.2 %   b) 47.9 %   c) 90.3 %   d) 45.32 %

12 0.587 as a percentage is 58.7 %   ◀ 0.587 is 58.7 ÷ 100, which is 58.7 %
    Write each decimal as a percentage.
    a) 0.435   b) 0.204   c) 0.991   d) 0.4532

13 Write each fraction and percentage as a decimal.
    Underline the larger number.
    a) 88 %; $\frac{7}{8}$ b) 93 %; $\frac{15}{16}$ c) 26 %; $\frac{21}{80}$ d) 48 %; $\frac{15}{32}$

14 0.333... as a percentage is 33.3... %   ◀ 0.333... is 33.333... ÷ 100, which is 33.333... %
    Write each decimal as a percentage.
    a) 0.666...   b) 0.111...   c) 0.717 171...   d) 0.121212...

15 Write each number as a decimal, as accurately as your
    calculator allows, then underline the larger number.
    a) $\frac{1}{3}$; 34 %   b) $\frac{2}{11}$; 18 %   c) $\frac{7}{9}$; 77 %   d) $\frac{7}{43}$; 16.5 %

16 $\frac{5}{36}$ of a bag of mixed fruit is raisins, and 15 % is chopped plums.
    Which is larger, the mass of raisins or the mass of plums?

1   Read the pets problem.
    To solve it we can compare percentages:
    9 out of 20 is 45 out of 100, or 45 %;
    12 out of 25 is 48 out of 100, or 48 %.
    So cats are more popular in Dell Avenue.

9 of the 20 families in Penn Lane have cats.
12 of the 25 families in Dell Avenue have cats.
In which road are cats more popular?

Another house in Penn Lane gets a pet cat.
Are cats still more popular in Dell Avenue?
Explain your answer.

2   a) What fraction of the circle is shaded?
    b) What fraction of the square is shaded?
    c) What percentage of the circle is shaded?
    d) What percentage of the square is shaded?
    e) Which has the larger proportion shaded,
       the circle or the square?

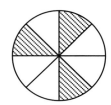
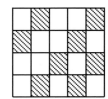

3   a) Look at the Sale notices.
       Which shop is giving the better saving?
       Explain your answer.

    b) Which is better:

       40 % extra Cola for the same price,
       or $\frac{5}{12}$ extra Cola for the same price?

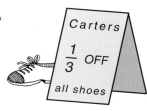

4   24 % of the fish in a tank are guppies.
    $\frac{7}{30}$ are angel fish.
    Are there more guppies or more angel fish?
    Explain your answer.

5   $\frac{3}{5}$ of a field is planted with potatoes and $\frac{1}{8}$ with peas.
    The remainder is planted with corn.

    a) Write the two fractions as percentages.
    b) What percentage of the field is planted with corn?
    c) What fraction of the field is planted with corn?

6   a) A survey shows that 12 out of 59 bikes have
       faulty lights.
       What percentage is this, correct to 2 DP ?
    b) 52 out of 256 cars have faulty lights.
       What percentage is this, correct to 2 DP ?
    c) Which had worse lights, the bikes or the cars?

7   On Monday Karen got 18 out of 25 in a science test.
    On Tuesday she got 38 out of 60 in a science test.
    Which test do you think was easier?
    Use percentages to explain your answer.

8   a) Pat's building society employs 8 women and 3 men.
       What percentage are women?
    b) Pat's bank employs 17 women and 8 men.
       What percentage are women?
    c) Which has a more even balance of women and men,
       the building society or the bank?

9   Anne is an Albion fan.
    The table shows how many home and away games she
    saw last season, and whether Albion won, drew or lost.
    a) How many games did Anne see altogether?
    b) What percentage of the games
        (i)   were at home
        (ii) were wins
        (iii) were away wins ?
    c) What percentage of the home games were wins?
    d) What percentage of the away games were wins?
    e) Do you think Albion were more successful in
       home games or away games?
       Explain your answer.

Albion games seen by Anne last season

	home	away
WIN	3	2
DRAW	5	3
LOSE	7	4

10 Last month for breakfast Rod had corn flakes 23 times and wheat flakes 7 times.
    He had strawberries with his corn flakes on 10 mornings and with his wheat flakes
    on 3 mornings.
    Do you think he prefers to have strawberries with corn flakes or with wheat flakes?
    Use percentages to explain your answer.

11 Umesh ran five 100 m and eight 200 m races last year.
    He won five races altogether, two of them at 100 m.
    a) What percentage (correct to 1 DP) of his races did
       he win?
    b) What percentage of his 100 m races did he win?
    c) Do you think Umesh runs better at 100 m or 200 m ?
       Explain your answer.

12 In a town, 2 in every 7 families have one child.
    3 in every 10 families have two children.
    5 in every 14 families have more than 2 children.
    a) Are there more families with one child, two
       children, or more than 2 children?
       Explain how you decided.
    b) Estimate the percentage of families which have
       no children.

Car puzzle
Meg has 50 model cars.
20 are VWs and 9 of these
are red.
Does she have a greater
percentage of cars that are
VWs or VWs that are red?

●●●●●●●●●●●●●●●●●●●●●●●●●●●●●

Do NOT use a calculator for Questions 1 - 8.

1   0.08 is $\frac{8}{100}$, which is $\frac{2}{25}$ as a fraction in its simplest form.

Write these decimals as fractions in their simplest form.
a) 0.06   b) 0.07   c) 0.4   d) 0.005   e) 0.0008   f) 0.9   g) 0.00002

2   0.27 is $\frac{2}{10} + \frac{7}{100}$, which is $\frac{20}{100} + \frac{7}{100}$, which is $\frac{27}{100}$.

Show that
a) 0.83 is $\frac{83}{100}$ b) 0.035 is $\frac{35}{1000}$ c) 0.208 is $\frac{208}{1000}$ d) 0.845 is $\frac{845}{1000}$.

3   Write these decimals as fractions in their simplest form.
a) 0.26   b) 0.56   c) 0.084   d) 0.206   e) 0.0025   f) 0.091   g) 0.125

4   $\frac{3}{5}$ is $\frac{6}{10}$, which is 0.6.

Write each fraction with a denominator 10, or 100, or 1000.
Use your result to write each fraction as a decimal.
a) $\frac{4}{5}$ b) $\frac{3}{20}$ c) $\frac{70}{200}$ d) $\frac{24}{25}$ e) $\frac{1}{50}$ f) $\frac{107}{250}$ g) $\frac{3}{200}$

5   Pam is finding $\frac{3}{8}$ as a decimal, without using a calculator.
She divides 3 by 8. ▶

$$\frac{3.\overset{3}{0}000}{8} = 0.$$

Look carefully at the steps she takes:

8 into 3 units is **0**, with 3 units left over.

$$\frac{3.\overset{3}{0}\overset{6}{0}00}{8} = 0.3$$

3 units is 30 tenths;
8 into 30 tenths is **3** tenths, with 6 tenths left over.

6 tenths is 60 hundredths.
8 into 60 hundredths is **7** hundredths, with 4 hundredths left over.

$$\frac{3.\overset{3}{0}\overset{6}{0}\overset{4}{0}0}{8} = 0.37$$

4 hundredths is 40 thousandths;
8 into 40 thousandths is **5** thousandths.

$$\frac{3.\overset{3}{0}\overset{6}{0}\overset{4}{0}0}{8} = 0.375$$

So $\frac{3}{8}$ is **0.375**.

Change these fractions into decimals.
Use Pam's method. Write divisions like this one.
a) $\frac{5}{8}$ b) $\frac{1}{8}$ c) $\frac{3}{4}$ d) $\frac{2}{5}$ e) $\frac{7}{20}$ f) $\frac{13}{20}$ g) $\frac{7}{50}$

6   Pam is changing $\frac{2}{7}$ into a decimal.
    a) Copy and continue her division;
        find the next eight digits.
    b) What do you notice about the result?

$$\frac{2.\overset{2}{0}\overset{6}{0}\overset{4}{0}\overset{5}{0}\overset{1}{0}0000}{7} = 0.2857$$

7   Think about the decimal for $\frac{2}{7}$ in Question 6.
    It is called a **recurring decimal**.
    The pattern of digits 285714 repeats itself forever.
    To show this we place a dot above the 2 and the 4. ▶

$$\frac{2}{7} = 0.\dot{2}8571\dot{4}$$

    Write these fractions as decimals.
    Use dots to show the repeating pattern of digits.
    a) $\frac{1}{7}$ b) $\frac{5}{7}$

8   The decimal for $\frac{5}{12}$ is the recurring decimal 0.4166666...
    The digit 6 is repeated forever.
    To show this we place a dot above the first 6. ▶

$$\frac{5}{12} = 0.41\dot{6}$$

    Write these fractions as decimals.
    Use a dot or dots to show the repeating digits.
    a) $\frac{1}{6}$ b) $\frac{4}{9}$ c) $\frac{4}{11}$

9   Look at the list of fractions.
    a) Write the list out in full.
    b) Tick (✓) the fractions that give recurring decimals.
        Use a calculator to help you decide.
    c) Think about the recurring decimals you ticked.
        What is special about their denominators?

| $\frac{1}{2}$ | $\frac{1}{3}$ | $\frac{1}{4}$ | $\frac{1}{5}$ | ... | ... | $\frac{1}{20}$ |

Decimal order
Look at these four decimals.

0.$\ddot{2}$0   0.$\ddot{0}$2   0.0$\dot{2}$ 0.$\dot{2}$

10 *Use a calculator.*

a. Write them in order, smallest
first.

    a) Check that $\frac{4}{33} = 0.\dot{1}\dot{2}$ and that $\frac{5}{33} = 0.\dot{1}\dot{5}$.
    b) Make some careful guesses.
        Find a fraction equal to
        (i) $0.\dot{1}\dot{8}$ (ii) $0.\dot{1}\dot{9}$.

b. Make careful guesses. Write
each decimal as a fraction. Use
your calculator to help you.

11 *Use a calculator where it is helpful.*
    Look at the fractions A - G.
    A $\frac{2}{3}$ B $\frac{6}{10}$ C $\frac{16}{25}$ D $\frac{11}{18}$ E $\frac{5}{8}$ F $\frac{33}{50}$ G $\frac{64}{99}$
    a) Write the fractions as decimals.
    b) Use your results in part a).
        Write the fractions A - G in order, smallest first.

1 Look at the fractions A - G.

A $\frac{3}{10}$ B $\frac{1}{4}$ C $\frac{49}{50}$ D $\frac{1}{2}$ E $\frac{12}{25}$ F $\frac{6}{200}$ G $\frac{14}{40}$

Do not use a calculator.
a) Write each fraction with denominator 100.
b) Write each fraction as a percentage.

2 Look at the fractions A - G.

A $\frac{3}{4}$ B $\frac{39}{60}$ C $\frac{2}{5}$ D $\frac{23}{50}$ E $\frac{7}{8}$ F $\frac{19}{40}$ G $\frac{41}{400}$

a) *Use a calculator (even if you don't really need to).*
   Write each fraction in decimal form.
b) Write each decimal as a percentage.   ◀ Careful! 0.4 is not 4 %. 0.875 is not 875 %.

3 Look at the decimals A - G.

A 0.14   B 0.04   C 0.8   D 0.349   E 0.303   F 0.0303   G 1.15

a) Write each decimal as a division by 100.
b) Use your results in part a) to write each
   decimal as a percentage.

Example: $0.345 = 34.5 \div 100$

Example: $34.5 \div 100 = 34.5\%$

4 Look at the decimals A - G.

A 0.125   B 0.0219   C 0.0041   D $0.\dot{3}$ E $0.\ddot{6}\dot{2}$ F $0.6\dot{2}$ G $0.8\ddot{2}\dot{3}$

Write each decimal as a percentage, correct to
a) the nearest whole number   b) 1 DP.

5 Look at the fractions A - G.

A $\frac{9}{10}$ B $\frac{2}{3}$ C $\frac{1}{9}$ D $\frac{7}{9}$ E $\frac{1}{16}$ F $\frac{3}{50}$ G $\frac{5}{7}$

Use a calculator where it is helpful.
a) Write each fraction as a decimal.
b) Use your results in part a) to write each fraction as
   a percentage, correct to the nearest whole number.

6 Look at the percentages A - G.

A 12.4 %   B 1.5 %   C 7.5 %   D 40.8 %   E 12.8 %   F 0.55 %   G 1.23 %

Write each percentage as
a) a decimal
b) a fraction in its simplest form.

Example: $23.5\% = 23.5 \div 100 = 0.235$

Example: $0.235 = \frac{235}{1000} = \frac{47}{200}$

7 Aysha says $\frac{1}{2}$ is bigger than 45 % because $\frac{1}{2}$ is 50 %.

Do not use a calculator.
Look at the pairs A - E.
For each pair, decide which fraction, decimal or percentage is the larger.
Give a reason each time.

A $\frac{1}{5}$ and 22 %   B $\frac{3}{4}$ and 0.69   C $\frac{17}{50}$ and 0.4   D 0.9 and 9 %   E $\frac{4}{9}$ and 51 %

8 *Do not use a calculator.*
Look at the sets A - D.
For each set, write the fraction, decimal and percentage in order, smallest first.

A $\frac{1}{2}$, 0.6, 35 %   B $\frac{11}{20}$, 0.5, 49 %   C $\frac{1}{90}$, 0.1, 1 %   D $\frac{999}{1000}$, 0.$\dot{9}$, 99 %

9 *Do not use a calculator.*
There are 20 questions in a test, with
1 mark each.
Rajan gets 5 questions correct.
Betty gets 5 % of the questions correct.
Lisa gets 0.5 of the questions correct.
Who does best on the test?
Explain your answer.

Brollybility
The chance of rain
tomorrow is 0.15.
Write the chance of
no rain tomorrow as
a. a fraction
b. a percentage.
●●●●●●●●●●●●●●●●●●●●●●●

10 *Do not use a calculator.*
Lynn, Zita and Ben share some cherries.
Lynn gets $\frac{1}{4}$ and Zita gets 0.4 of the cherries.
a) Write Ben's share as a percentage.
b) Who gets the largest share, Lynn, Zita or Ben?

11 *Do not use a calculator.*
A 200 g portion of beans contains 13.4 g of protein.
Write the amount of protein as
a) a percentage   b) a fraction.

12 *Use a calculator.*
   a) A 60 g serving of Muesli contains 3.7 g of fibre.
       What percentage is fibre, to the nearest whole number?
   b) A 30 g serving of Rice Pops contains 0.2 g of fibre.
       What fraction is fibre?
   c) A 37.5 g serving of Wheatabix contains 3.8 g fibre.
       What decimal fraction is fibre?
   d) Which has most fibre, 100 g of Muesli, Rice Pops or
       Wheatabix?

Clear signal
Signal toothpaste
contains 0.32 % of
sodium fluoride.
Write this as
a. a fraction
b. a decimal.
●●●●●●●●●●●●●●●●●●●●●●●

13 *Use a calculator.*
   a) Pantone 363 is a green colour made by mixing 14 parts yellow, 2 parts red and 1 part black.
      Write the amount of black as
      (i) a fraction   (ii) a decimal (correct to 2 SF)   (iii) a percentage (correct to 2 SF).
   b) Pantone 2603 is a purple colour made by mixing 8 parts red, 8 parts violet and $\frac{1}{2}$ part black.
      Write the amount of black as
      (i) a fraction   (ii) a decimal (correct to 2 SF)   (iii) a percentage (correct to 2 SF).

14 Copy and complete the table.

fraction	$\frac{11}{20}$	$\frac{1}{9}$				
decimal			0.67	0.124		
percentage					26.5	7.18

1   The rectangle has 3 parts blue and 5 parts white. ▶
    We say that the *ratio* of blue parts to white parts
    is '3 to 5'.
    We write '3 to 5' as 3 : 5.

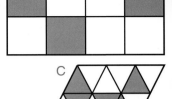

What is the ratio
of blue parts to
white parts in each
of these shapes?

A 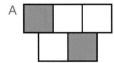   B   C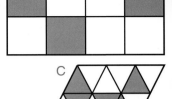

2   A jar contains 5 green marbles, 4 blue marbles
    and 7 red marbles.
    The ratio of blue marbles to red marbles is 4 : 7.

What is the ratio of
a) red marbles to blue marbles?
b) green marbles to blue marbles?
c) red marbles to non-red marbles?

3   For the rectangle, the ratio
    length : width is 9 : 4.
    What is the ratio
    a) length : perimeter
    b) width : perimeter ?

9 cm

4 cm

4   The ratio of the areas of the
    two squares is 4 : 9.
    a) Write down the lengths
        of sides of the two squares.
    b) Write down the ratio of
        the lengths of sides.

Area
= 4 cm²

Area
= 9 cm²

5   The masses of two loaves are 513 g and 1.5 kg.
    So the masses are 513 g and 1500 g, and the ratio of their
    masses is 513 : 1500.
    To find ratios we must use the same units for both quantities.

Find the ratio of each pair of quantities.
a) 29 g; 0.3 kg   b) 3 cm; 9 mm   c) 23 ml; 1.2 *l*   d) 3.4 m; 3.4 km

6   a) The lengths of two pieces of metal pipe are 1.2 m and 191 cm.
        Write down the ratio of the lengths of the two pieces.
    b) Jim cuts the shorter pipe into two pieces, one 84 cm long.
        Write down the ratio of the lengths of the two pieces.

7 a) The ratio of the lengths of sides of two squares is 3 : 8.
      What is the ratio of the areas of the squares?
   b) The ratio of the areas of two squares is 16 : 25.
      What is the ratio of the lengths of sides of the squares?

8 The scale on a town map is 1 : 5000.
   So 1 cm on the map represents 5000 cm in real life.
   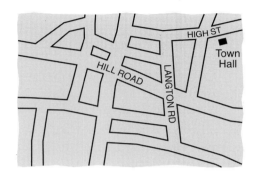
   a) On the map Langton Road is 3 cm long.
      How many metres long is Langton Road?
   b) The Town Hall and the Railway Station are
      1 km apart.
      How many cm is this on the map?
   c) On another map Tardis Road is 7.5 cm long.
      In real life Tardis Road is 150 m long.
      Write the scale of the map as a ratio.

9 a) Look at plate A.
      For each black bean there are 2 blue beans.
      Write a similar sentence for plate B.
   b) Draw a plate which has 4 black beans, and for
      which the ratio black beans : blue beans is 1 : 2.

   A    B

   c) The ratios of black beans to blue beans for
      plates A and B can be written as 2 : 4 and 3 : 6.
      Both of these are equivalent to 1 : 2, because on
      each plate there is one black bean for every two
      blue beans.
      We can write   1 : 2 = 2 : 4 = 3 : 6.
      1 : 2, 2 : 4 and 3 : 6 are called **equivalent ratios**.

      Write another ratio equivalent to 1 : 2.
   d) Write a ratio equivalent to 3 : 4.

10 We can produce equivalent ratios
    by multiplying or dividing each
    number in the ratio by the same
    number. ▶

    Examples:
    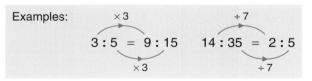

    Write a ratio equivalent to
    a) 2 : 3   b) 5 : 4   c) 7 : 10   d) 32 : 38   e) 1.2 : 3   f) 2.6 : 3.3

11 4 : 5 is equivalent to 1 : 1.25.
    Write each of these ratios in the form 1 : ☐.

    Example:
    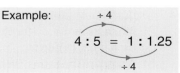

    a) 4 : 12   b) 3 : 27   c) 2 : 8   d) 8 : 2
    e) 5 : 1   f) 3.5 : 7   g) 0.2 : 3   h) 0.4 : 6

12 Look at the rectangle.
    Write these ratios in
    the form 1 : ☐.
    a) width : length
    b) width : perimeter
    c) length : perimeter.

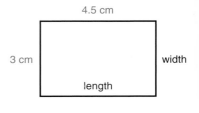

13 A working drawing of the plan of a house uses
    the scale 1 : 50.
    A second working drawing for the same house
    uses the scale 1 : 100.
    Which drawing do you think is easier to read?
    Explain your answer.

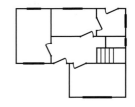

14 We can use ratios to make comparisons.

    Example: Tammy and Brian are mixing mortar to build a wall.
                Tammy uses 2 parts cement to 5 parts sand.
                Brian uses 3 parts cement to 7 parts sand.
                The mixture with less sand tends to be harder.
                Whose mixture will be harder?

    Solution: The cement : sand ratios are
                 Tammy 1 : 2.5   Brian 1 : 2.333…
                 Brian uses less sand to each part of cement,
                 so his mixture will be harder.

    Which of these cement : sand mixes will be harder?
     a) 4 : 7 or 5 : 9   b) 2 : 5 or 5 : 12   c) 3 : 5 or 5 : 8

15 a) Darren mixes tins of black paint and white paint in the ratio 2 : 9.
        Write the ratio in the form 1 : ☐.
    b) Peggy mixes tins of black paint and white paint in the ratio 5 : 23.
        Write the ratio in the form 1 : ☐.
    c) Compare the ratios. Whose paint mixture is lighter?
    d) Write down a ratio 1 : ☐ which gives a lighter grey than Darren's
        but a darker grey than Peggy's.
    e) Write your ratio in part d) using whole numbers.

16 Kate uses 2 tablespoonfuls of sugar to every 5 litres
    of lemon juice she makes.
    Jed uses 5 tablespoonfuls to every 8 litres he makes.
    a) Write the ratio,
        number of tablespoonfuls : number of litres,
        in the form 1 : ☐ for the juice made by
        (i) Kate   (ii) Jed.
    b) Compare the ratios. Whose lemon juice is sweeter?

Years to years
Aylish is 15 years old
and David is 5 years old.
a. Write down the ratio,
in the form ☐ : 1, of
their ages
i. now
ii. in 15 years time.
b. After how many
years will the ratio be
9 : 7 ?

30

17 Marco makes a salad dressing by mixing vinegar
and oil in the ratio 5 : 8.
a) Write the ratio vinegar : oil in the form 1 : ☐.
b) How much oil does Marco need if he uses
    100 ml of vinegar?
c) Write the ratio oil : vinegar in the form 1 : ☐.
d) How much vinegar does Marco need if he uses
    100 ml of oil?

18 a) The ratio of the heights of two trees is 2 : 5.
       Write the ratio height of smaller tree : height of taller tree
       in the form 1 : ☐.
    b) If the smaller tree is 3 m tall, how tall is the taller tree?
    c) Write the ratio height of taller tree : height of smaller tree
       in the form 1 : ☐.
    d) If the larger tree is 3 m tall, how tall is the smaller tree?

19 Write the ratio
    mass of the orange : mass of the grapefruit
    in the form
    a) 220 : ☐   b) 1 : ☐.

220 g   704 g

20 For a recipe Meg needs to divide 240 g of flour into two
    piles in the ratio 3 : 5. ▶
    3 : 5 means 3 equal parts in the smaller pile, and 5 equal
    equal parts in the larger pile - 8 equal parts altogether.
    So each part is 240 g ÷ 8 = 30 g.
    So the piles are 90 g and 150 g.

3 : 5

    Divide these amounts into the given ratios.
    a) 16 kg; 3 : 5   b) 20 kg; 4 : 1   c) 24 ml; 1 : 2   d) 40 cm; 2 : 3
    e) 70 km; 3 : 4   f) 60 cl; 7 : 5   g) 64 m; 9 : 7   h) 120 m; 3 : 17

21 The perimeter of a rectangle is 56 cm.
    The ratio of the width to the length is 3 : 4.
    How wide and how long is the rectangle?

22 a) At the end of the hockey season the ratio of games won to games
       lost by Blackway United is 4 : 1.
       During the season, Blackway played 44 games, drawing 4 of them.
       How many games did they win, and how many did they lose?
    b) Charlford Rovers also played 44 games.
       The ratio games won : games drawn : games lost was 4 : 5 : 2.
       How many games did Charlford win, draw and lose?

1 Look at the **sequence** of numbers. ▶
   The **first term** of the sequence is 8.
   The **second term** is 11.

8, 11, 14, 17, 20, ..., ...

◀ In a **sequence**
  • the numbers go on forever
  • the numbers follow a pattern.

   Write down
   a) the 6th term   b) the 7th term.

2 Look at the sequences A, B and C.
   Write down the 6th and 7th term of
   each sequence.

A   2, 8, 14, 20, 26, ..., ...
B   9, 21, 33, 45, 57, ..., ...
C   200, 188, 176, 164, 152, ..., ...

3 The 50th term of this sequence is 103.
   Write down the
   a) 51st term b) 53rd term c) 49th term.

5, 7, 9, 11, 13, ..., ...

4 Look at the four dot patterns.
   The numbers of dots form a sequence.
   a) Draw the 5th dot pattern.
   b) How many dots does the
       5th pattern have?
   c) Imagine the 6th pattern.
       How many dots does it have?

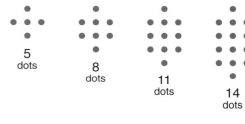

5
dots

8
dots

11
dots

14
dots

5 Look at the sequence of dot patterns.
   a) Imagine the 5th pattern.
       How many dots does it have?
   b) Imagine the 6th pattern.
       How many dots does it have?

6 Look at the sequences A, B, C and D.
   Sequence A is an 'Add 6' sequence. ▶
   6 is added each time to give the next term.

A   1, 7, 13, 19, 25, ..., ...
B   4, 9, 13, 18, 23, ..., ...
C   2, 10, 18, 26, 34, ..., ...
D   8, 17, 26, 35, 44, ..., ...

   a) Copy then complete.
       Sequence B is an '...... sequence'.
       Sequence C is an '...... sequence'.
   b) Describe sequence D.
   c) The 20th term of sequence A is 115.
       What is the 21st term?
   d) The 50th term of sequence B is 249.
       What is the 49th term?
   e) The 30th term of sequence C is 234.
       What is the 28th term?
   f) The 43rd term of sequence D is 386.
       What is the 45th term?

7   Look at the sequences. ▶
    Sequence A is an 'Add 5' sequence.
    To get the 3rd term we start with 1, then add 5 twice.
    So the 3rd term is $1 + (2 \times 5)$, or 11.

    A   1, 6, 11, 16, 21, ..., ...
    B   2, 5, 8, 11, 14, ..., ...
    C   5, 11, 17, 23, 29, ..., ...

    a) Copy then complete for sequence B:
       To get the 3rd term we start with ...,
       then add ... twice.
       So the 3rd term is $... + (... \times 3)$, or 8.
    b) Copy then complete this for the 3rd term
       of sequence C: $... + (... \times 6) = 17$.
    c) Copy then complete this for the 4th term
       of sequence A: $1 + (... \times 5) = 16$.
    d) Write the 4th term of B in the same way.
    e) Write the 4th term of C in the same way.
    f) Copy then complete this for the 10th term
       of sequence A: $1 + (... \times 5) = ...$
    g) Calculate the 10th term of sequence B.
    h) Calculate the 10th term of sequence C.

8   Look at the sequence of dot patterns.
    a) Imagine the 5th pattern.
       How many *more* dots does it have
       than the 4th pattern?
    b) Imagine the 10th pattern.
       Copy then complete for the number
       of dots: $2 + (... \times ...) = ...$
    c) Work out the number of dots in the
       20th pattern.

9   This is a 'Subtract 4' sequence. ▶

    100, 96, 92, 88, ..., ...

    a) The 3rd term is $100 - (2 \times 4) = 92$.
       Write the 4th term in the same way.
    b) Write the 5th term in the same way.
    c) Copy and complete for the 10th term:
       $100 - (... \times 4) = ...$
    d) Calculate the 20th term.

10 5, 7, 9, 11, 13, ..., ... is an 'Add 2' sequence.
    a) Copy then complete to find the 8th term: $... + (... \times ...) = ...$
    b) Copy then complete to find the 50th term: $... + (... \times ...) = ...$

11 Look at this 'Add 9' sequence. ▶
    Which term do you get if you

    2, 11, 20, 29, 38, ..., ...

    a) multiply 3 by 9, then add 2
    b) multiply 30 by 9, then add 2
    c) multiply 30 by 9, then subtract 7 ?

12 Look at the 'tables and chairs' patterns.
    a) List the next 3 terms of the number sequence
        for chairs: 4, 6, 8, …
    b) Copy then complete to find the number of chairs
        needed for 12 tables: … + (… × …) = …
    c) How many chairs are needed for 20 tables?

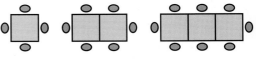

1 table   2 tables   3 tables
4 chairs   6 chairs   8 chairs

13 This is the sequence of whole numbers. ▶
    Many sequences are produced from it
    by multiplying (or dividing) each term
    then adding (or subtracting) a number.
    For example, sequence A is made from
    it by multiplying by 4 then adding 2. ▶

1, 2, 3, 4, 5, …

multiply by 4
then add 2

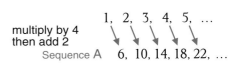

1, 2, 3, 4, 5, …

Sequence A   6, 10, 14, 18, 22, …

    a) To find the 12th term of sequence A,
        you multiply 12 by 4 then add 2.
        Write down the 12th term.
    b) Find the 16th term of sequence A.
    c) 82 is a term in the sequence.
        What is its position?
        Explain how you decided.
    d) Find the 100th term.
    e) What position is 802 in the sequence?

14 This sequence is made from the sequence of whole
    numbers by subtracting 1 then multiplying by 3. ▶

subtract 1 then
multiply by 3

1, 2, 3, 4, 5, …

0, 3, 6, 9, 12, …

    a) Subtract 1 then multiply by 3 to find
        (i) the 15th term   (ii) the 60th term.
    b) What position in the sequence is the term 237 ?

15 a) Copy then complete the sequence descriptions.

A   1, 2, 3, 4, 5, …   B   1, 2, 3, 4, 5, …
subtract … then   multiply by …
multiply by …   0, 2, 4, 6, 8, …   2, 4, 6, 8, 10, …

C   1, 2, 3, 4, 5, …   D   1, 2, 3, 4, 5, …
multiply by …   multiply by …
then add …   3, 5, 7, 9, 11, …   then subtract …   1, 3, 5, 7, 9, …

E   1, 2, 3, 4, 5, …   F   1, 2, 3, 4, 5, …
… 1 then … 3   … 4 then … 5
                   6, 9, 12, 15, 18, …   25, 30, 35, 40, 45, …

    b) Find the 20th term of each sequence.
    c) Find the 50th term of each sequence.

16 a) Describe how each sequence is produced
   from the whole number sequence
   (eg, multiply by 2; multiply by 2 then add 3).
   (Hint: When you are finding the rules for B, D
   and F compare the sequences with A, C and E.)

A   1, 2, 3, 4, 5, ...
     ↓ ↓ ↓ ↓ ↓
     4, 8, 12, 16, 20, ...

B   1, 2, 3, 4, 5, ...
     ↓ ↓ ↓ ↓ ↓
     5, 9, 13, 17, 21, ...

C   1, 2, 3, 4, 5, ...
     ↓ ↓ ↓ ↓ ↓
     3, 6, 9, 12, 15, ...

D   1, 2, 3, 4, 5, ...
     ↓ ↓ ↓ ↓ ↓
     2, 5, 8, 11, 14, ...

E   1, 2, 3, 4, 5, ...
     ↓ ↓ ↓ ↓ ↓
     5, 10, 15, 20, 25, ...

F   1, 2, 3, 4, 5, ...
     ↓ ↓ ↓ ↓ ↓
     7, 12, 17, 22, 27, ...

b) Find the 20th term of each sequence.
c) Find the 50th term of each sequence.

17 In this whole number sequence ▶
   the nth term has been included.
   n can be any number we wish.
   To find each term of sequence A
   we multiply by 6. ▶
   So the nth term of sequence A
   is $6 \times n$, or $6n$.

1, 2, 3, 4, ..., n, ...

1, 2, 3, 4, ..., n, ...
multiply by 6   ↓ ↓ ↓ ↓   ↓
Sequence A   6, 12, 18, 24, ..., $6n$, ...

a) Copy then complete each diagram.

A   1, 2, 3, 4, ..., n, ...
multiply by ... ↓ ↓ ↓ ↓   ↓
               7, 14, 21, 28, ..., $7n$, ...

B   1, 2, 3, 4, ..., n, ...
multiply by ... ↓ ↓ ↓ ↓   ↓
               9, 18, 27, 36, ..., $?n$, ...

C   1, 2, 3, 4, ..., n, ...
multiply by ... ↓ ↓ ↓ ↓   ↓
then add 1   5, 9, 13, 17, ..., $?n + 1$, ...

D   1, 2, 3, 4, ..., n, ...
multiply by 4 ↓ ↓ ↓ ↓   ↓
then subtract ... 2, 6, 10, 14, ..., $4n - ?$, ...

E   1, 2, 3, 4, ..., n, ...
add ... then   ↓ ↓ ↓ ↓   ↓
multiply by 2 6, 8, 10, 12, ..., $2(n + ?)$, ...

F   1, 2, 3, 4, ..., n, ...
subtract ... then ↓ ↓ ↓ ↓   ↓
multiply by 5 0, 5, 10, 15, ..., $5(n - ?)$, ...

b) Find the 50th term of each sequence.
c) Find the 100th term of each sequence.

18 Rules P, Q and R give the nth term of three sequences.
    List the first five terms of each sequence.

    Rule P

    Take 1 from n,
    multiply the result by 6,
    then add 2.

    Rule Q

    Take 1 from n,
    multiply the result by 10,
    then add 25.

    Rule R

    Take 1 from n,
    multiply the result by 3,
    then subtract from 30.

19 Look at this 'Add 7' sequence.   4, 11, 18, 25, 32, ..., ...
    a) Write a rule, like P, Q and R in Q 18,
        for the nth term of the sequence.
    b) Use your rule.
        (i) Check that the 5th term is 32.
        (ii) Find the 21st term.

20 Look at the sequences A, B and C.   A 1, 5, 9, 13, 17, ..., ...
    Write a rule for the nth term of each   B 22, 25, 28, 31, 34, ..., ...
    sequence.   C 55, 51, 47, 43, 39, ..., ...

21 a) The 3rd term of an 'Add 5' sequence is 19.
        (i) Find the first term.
        (ii) Write down a rule for the nth term.
        (iii) Use your rule to find the 50th term.
    b) The 2nd term of an 'Add a number' sequence
        is 21. The 4th term is 29.
        (i) Find the first term.
        (ii) Write down a rule for the nth term.
        (iii) Write down a rule for the kth term.

> **Special sequence**
> This is *not* an 'Add
> a number' sequence:
> 2, 5, 10, 17, 26, ...
> a. Find the 6th term.
> b. Try to find a rule
> for the nth term.

22 Look at the 'rectangles and sticks' patterns.
    a) Work out how many sticks are needed
        for 8 rectangles.
    b) Write a rule for the number of sticks
        needed for d rectangles.
    c) How many sticks are needed for $d = 12$?

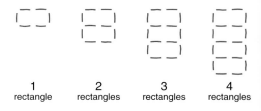

| 1 | 2 | 3 | 4 |
| rectangle | rectangles | rectangles | rectangles |

23 Look at the cross patterns.
    a) The single cross has a perimeter of 12 units.
        Check that the 2-cross pattern has a perimeter
        of 18 units.
    b) What is the perimeter of the 3-cross pattern?
    c) Write down a rule for the perimeter of the
        k-cross pattern.
    d) What is the perimeter when $k = 100$?

36

1   Angie adds a number to 4.
    The result is 9.
    This **equation** shows what she did: $4 + x = 9$.
    x must be 5.
    We say that the **solution** to the equation is $x = 5$.

    Write down the solutions to these equations.
    You will be able to solve each one by thinking:
    'What number added to ...... gives ......?'
    a) $4 + x = 7$ b) $1 + x = 8$ c) $3 + x = 5$
    d) $2 + x = 12$ e) $x + 4 = 6$ f) $x + 7 = 9$
    g) $x + 1 = 10$ h) $x + 5 = 13$ i) $x + 9 = 16$
    j) $x + 4 = 19$ k) $x + 7 = 20$ l) $x + 11 = 30$

2   Write down an equation, ... + ... = ... , whose solution is
    a) $x = 10$ b) $x = 11$ c) $x = 14$.

3   This equation involves a subtraction: $7 - x = 3$.
    To solve it, we think: What number subtracted from 7 gives 3 ?
    The solution is $x = 4$.

    Solve these equations.
    a) $8 - x = 7$ b) $6 - x = 2$ c) $7 - x = 5$
    d) $5 - x = 4$ e) $4 - x = 0$ f) $5 - x = 5$
    g) $9 - x = 7$ h) $12 - x = 3$ i) $16 - x = 10$
    j) $17 - x = 12$ k) $20 - x = 2$ l) $20 - x = 7$

4   Write down an equation, ... $- x =$ ...... , whose solution is
    a) $x = 10$ b) $x = 11$ c) $x = 15$.

5   In this equation a number is subtracted from x: $x - 5 = 3$.
    To solve it, we think: What number do I subtract 5 from to leave 3 ?
    The solution is $x = 8$.

    Solve these equations.
    a) $x - 1 = 3$ b) $x - 2 = 3$ c) $x - 3 = 3$
    d) $x - 4 = 2$ e) $x - 4 = 1$ f) $x - 4 = 4$
    g) $x - 5 = 4$ h) $x - 7 = 3$ i) $x - 9 = 3$
    j) $x - 7 = 7$ k) $x - 6 = 0$ l) $x - 2 = 12$

6   Write down an equation, $x -$ ...... = ... , whose solution is
    a) $x = 5$ b) $x = 6$ c) $x = 8$.

7   This equation tells us that $4 \times$ a number is 12: $4x = 12$.
The number must be 3.
The solution is $x = 3$.

Solve these equations.
a) $2x = 8$ b) $2x = 6$ c) $2x = 12$ d) $3x = 12$
e) $3x = 18$ f) $4x = 16$ g) $4x = 0$ h) $5x = 5$
i) $8x = 40$ j) $10x = 90$ k) $2x = 1$ l) $5x = 1$

8   Write down an equation, $...... x = ...$, whose solution is
a) $x = 7$ b) $x = 11$ c) $x = 1.5$

9   This equation tells us that 3 added to $2x$ gives 9: $2x + 3 = 9$.
$2x$ must be 6.
So x must be 3.
The solution is $x = 3$.

Think in the same way to solve these equations.
(First decide what $2x$ must be, then decide upon the value of x.)
a) $2x + 5 = 9$ b) $2x + 3 = 7$ c) $2x + 1 = 9$
d) $6 + 2x = 10$ e) $1 + 2x = 9$ f) $4 + 2x = 5$
g) $2x - 1 = 5$ h) $2x - 2 = 4$ i) $2x - 3 = 5$
j) $6 - 2x = 0$ k) $8 - 2x = 6$ l) $12 - 2x = 4$

10   Write down an equation, $2x + ... = ...$, whose solution is
a) $x = 1$ b) $x = 8$ c) $x = 1.5$

11   Solve these equations. (First decide what $3x$, $4x$, ... must be, then decide upon the value of x.)
a) $3x + 1 = 7$ b) $3x + 3 = 9$ c) $4x + 1 = 9$
d) $4x + 2 = 14$ e) $5x + 1 = 16$ f) $5x + 4 = 24$
g) $3x - 1 = 5$ h) $3x - 2 = 10$ i) $4x - 3 = 13$
j) $4x - 4 = 0$ k) $5x - 2 = 3$ l) $6x - 3 = 21$
m) $6 + 4x = 10$ n) $1 + 3x = 10$ o) $4 + 5x = 19$
p) $6 - 3x = 0$ q) $8 - 4x = 4$ r) $16 - 5x = 1$

12   This equation means that a number divided by 3 gives the result 7: $\frac{x}{3} = 7$.
The number must be 21.
So $x = 21$.

Solve these equations. (Think: 'What number divided by $......$ gives $......$?')
a) $\frac{x}{2} = 3$ b) $\frac{x}{2} = 6$ c) $\frac{x}{2} = 9$ d) $\frac{x}{3} = 3$

e) $\frac{x}{3} = 4$ f) $\frac{x}{3} = 6$ g) $\frac{x}{4} = 3$ h) $\frac{x}{5} = 2$

i) $\frac{x}{6} = 2$ j) $\frac{x}{5} = 5$ k) $\frac{x}{6} = 10$ l) $\frac{x}{8} = 1$

13 Write down an equation, $\dfrac{x}{...} = ...$, whose solution is

   a) $x = 20$ b) $x = 30$ c) $x = 26$.

---

14 This equation tells you that a number divides into 12 to give the result 2: $\dfrac{12}{x} = 2$.
    The number must be 6.
    So $x = 6$.

   Solve these equations. (Think: 'What number divides into ...... to give ......?')

   a) $\dfrac{4}{x} = 2$ b) $\dfrac{6}{x} = 2$ c) $\dfrac{8}{x} = 2$ d) $\dfrac{12}{x} = 3$

   e) $\dfrac{9}{x} = 3$ f) $\dfrac{12}{x} = 6$ g) $\dfrac{12}{x} = 4$ h) $\dfrac{20}{x} = 10$

   i) $\dfrac{20}{x} = 2$ j) $\dfrac{24}{x} = 6$ k) $\dfrac{24}{x} = 4$ l) $\dfrac{28}{x} = 4$

---

15 Write down an equation, $\dfrac{...}{x} = ...$, whose solution is

   a) $x = 7$ b) $x = 10$ c) $x = 100$.

---

16 In this equation, 3 added to $\dfrac{x}{2}$ gives 7: $\dfrac{x}{2} + 3 = 7$.
    So $\dfrac{x}{2}$ must be 4.
    So x must be 8.

   Solve these equations. (First decide what $\dfrac{x}{...}$ must be, then decide upon the value of x.)

   a) $\dfrac{x}{2} + 4 = 7$ b) $\dfrac{x}{2} + 3 = 8$ c) $\dfrac{x}{2} + 4 = 5$ d) $3 + \dfrac{x}{2} = 7$

   e) $3 + \dfrac{x}{2} = 8$ f) $5 + \dfrac{x}{2} = 9$ g) $\dfrac{x}{3} + 1 = 7$ h) $\dfrac{x}{3} - 2 = 4$

   i) $\dfrac{x}{5} - 2 = 1$ j) $3 + \dfrac{x}{3} = 4$ k) $8 - \dfrac{x}{2} = 7$ l) $3 - \dfrac{x}{5} = 2$

---

17 This equation tells us that 2 times $(x + 3)$ is 8: $2(x + 3) = 8$.
    So $(x + 3)$ must be 4.
    So x must be 1.

   Think in a similar way to solve these equations.

   a) $2(x + 1) = 8$ b) $2(x + 4) = 12$ c) $2(x - 1) = 8$

   d) $2(x - 3) = 8$ e) $3(x + 1) = 12$ f) $3(x - 1) = 6$

   g) $3(6 - x) = 12$ h) $4(7 - x) = 16$ i) $2(\dfrac{x}{5} - 3) = 8$

   j) $3(\dfrac{x}{2} + 1) = 15$ k) $3(\dfrac{4}{x} - 1) = 9$ l) $2(6 - \dfrac{x}{3}) = 10$

1   Look at the equation.

$$\frac{18}{x+4} = 2$$

As with many equations, we can solve it by trial and improvement, or by inspection.

Try $x = 2$: $\frac{18}{2+4} = 2$? … No

Try $x = 3$: $\frac{18}{3+4} = 2$? … No

Try $x = 5$: $\frac{18}{5+4} = 2$? … Yes.

Think: '$(x+4)$ divides into 18 to give 2'.
So $x + 4$ must be 9.
So $x = 5$.

Solve these equations.
Use trial and improvement, or inspection.

a) $4(x+3) = 16$

b) $8 + 6y = 32$

c) $5(8-x) = 10$

d) $2 + 12k = 38$

e) $6b + 4 = 28$

f) $50 = 60 - 2n$

g) $\frac{e+5}{2} = 14$

h) $\frac{10}{x-3} = 5$

i) $\frac{14}{p+9} = 1$

j) $2(7x+5) = 52$

k) $5n + 2 = 3n + 10$

l) $3(x+1) = x + 15$

---

2   Equations like $2x + 6 = x + 20$ are often difficult to solve by trial and improvement, or by inspection. So we first change them into a simpler equation.

We can think of the equation as a balance. Removing x from both sides leaves the amounts still balanced.
So $x + 6 = 20$.
So $x = 14$.

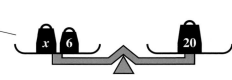

We write: $2x + 6 = x + 20$
Subtract x: $x + 6 = 20$
(Subtract 6): $x = 14$.

We can write 'Subtract 6', or simply use inspection to see that $x = 14$.

Solve these equations by first subtracting x from both sides.
a) $2x + 1 = x + 10$

b) $3x + 6 = x + 22$

c) $x + 17 = 2x + 8$

d) $2 + 6x = x + 12$

e) $5 + 3x = x + 21$

f) $7 + 3x = 21 + x$

g) $5 + 2x = x + 32$

h) $4 + 2x = 2 + x$

---

3   We can subtract any amount or value from both sides in order to solve an equation.
For example: Solve the equation $5x + 2 = 3x + 10$.

Solution: $5x + 2 = 3x + 10$
Subtract $3x$: $2x + 2 = 10$
(Subtract 2): $2x = 8$
(Divide by 2): $x = 4$.

We can write 'Subtract 2', or simply note by inspection that $2x = 8$.

We can write 'Divide by 2', or simply use inspection to see that $x = 4$.

Solve these equations by first subtracting …… x from both sides.
a) $4x + 1 = 3x + 13$

b) $3x + 6 = 2x + 16$

c) $4x + 9 = 2x + 17$

d) $2 + 6x = 5x + 16$

e) $3 + 4x = 2x + 27$

f) $18 + 7x = 4 + 5x$

g) $38 + 7x = 12x + 8$

h) $7 + 4x = 3 + 2x$

4   Sometimes it is better to *add* amounts or values to
    both sides to simplify the equation.
    For example: Solve the equation $5x - 2 = 14 - 3x$.

Solution: $5x - 2 = 14 - 3x$
Add $3x$: $8x - 2 = 14$
(Add 2): $8x = 16$
(Divide by 8): $x = 2.$

Solve these equations.
a) $x - 1 = 11 - 2x$ b) $2x - 5 = 15 - 3x$ c) $4x - 14 = 1 - x$
d) $3 - x = 8 - 2x$ e) $6 - x = 18 - 3x$ f) $4 - 3x = 10 - 2x$
g) $3 - 5x = 6 - 2x$ h) $4x - 1 = 11 - 2x$ i) $3x - 1 = 6 - 4x$

5   To solve equations like $3(x + 2) - 4 = x + 6$ we need
    first to multiply out the brackets.

Solution: $3(x + 2) - 4 = x + 6$
Multiply out the brackets: $3x + 6 - 4 = x + 6$
Simplify the left hand side: $3x + 2 = x + 6$
Subtract x: $2x + 2 = 6$
(Subtract 2): $2x = 4$
(Divide by 2): $x = 2.$

Solve these equations.
First multiply out the brackets.
a) $3(x - 3) = 2x + 2$ b) $4(x - 3) = x + 6$ c) $4(x + 3) = 3x - 2$
d) $5x - 11 = 2(x - 1)$ e) $2x + 8 = 4(x + 1)$ f) $5(x - 1) = 3x + 2$
g) $2(x + 1) - 3 = x + 4$ h) $3(x - 2) - 4 = x + 3$ i) $6(x + 2) + 5 = 3x + 20$
j) $26 - x = 3(x + 6)$ k) $3(x + 2) - 4 = 5x - 6$ l) $8x - 7 = 3(x + 1)$

6   Equations like $2(x + 3) - 4 = 2 + 4(x - 5)$ have brackets
    on both sides.

Solution: $2(x + 3) - 4 = 2 + 4(x - 5)$
Multiply out the brackets: $2x + 6 - 4 = 2 + 4x - 20$
Simplify each side: $2x + 2 = 4x - 18$
Subtract $2x$: $2 = 2x - 18$
(Add 18): $20 = 2x$
(Divide by 2): $x = 10.$

Solve these equations.
First multiply out the brackets.
a) $3(x - 3) - 4 = 2(x - 2)$ b) $3(x + 3) + 1 = 2(x + 5)$
c) $4(x + 3) = 6 + 2(3x - 5)$ d) $1 + 5(x - 3) = 3(2x - 1)$
e) $6 + 2(x - 3) = 4(x + 5)$ f) $2(x + 3) = 2 + 4(x - 5)$
g) $2(x - 3) - 4 = 2 + 4(x - 2)$ h) $2(x + 3) + 4 = 3 + 2(2x - 5)$
i) $4(x + 3) + 1 = 8 + 3(2x - 5)$ j) $6 + 5(x - 3) = 3(2x - 1)$
k) $2(x - 6) + 1 = 3(4x - 5)$ l) $8(x - 2) = 6(2x - 1)$

7   In an equation like $\frac{x}{3} + 9 = 4 + x$ it is useful first
to multiply both sides by the denominator 3.

Solution: $\frac{x}{3} + 9 = 4 + x$

Multiply by 3: $3(\frac{x}{3} + 9) = 3(4 + x)$
Multiply out the brackets: $x + 27 = 12 + 3x$
Subtract x: $27 = 12 + 2x$
(Subtract 12): $15 = 2x$
(Divide by 2): $x = 7.5$

Solve these equations.

a) $12 + \frac{x}{2} = 2 + x$ b) $\frac{x}{3} - 5 = 3 - x$ c) $x - 5 = 1 - \frac{x}{2}$ d) $3 - \frac{x}{2} = x - 3$

e) $3 - \frac{x}{5} = x - 9$ f) $10 - x = 4 - \frac{x}{3}$ g) $\frac{x}{4} - 1 = 17 - 2x$ h) $2x - 1 = 11 - \frac{x}{3}$

8   In equations like $\frac{12 + x}{2} = 2 + x$ again it is useful
first to multiply both sides by the denominator 2.

Solution: $\frac{12 + x}{2} = 2 + x$

Multiply by 2: $12 + x = 2(2 + x)$
Multiply out the brackets: $12 + x = 4 + 2x$
Subtract x: $12 = 4 + x$
(Subtract 4): $x = 8$

Solve these equations.

a) $\frac{12 + x}{3} = 2 + x$ b) $\frac{x - 5}{4} = 5 - x$ c) $x - 1 = \frac{1 - x}{2}$

d) $3 - 2x = \frac{2x - 7}{3}$ e) $3 - x = \frac{2x - 7}{2}$ f) $\frac{10 + 3x}{2} = 12 - 2x$

g) $\frac{x - 1}{3} = 9 - x$ h) $\frac{4x - 1}{3} = 2x - 1$ i) $3x - 1 = \frac{1 - 4x}{2}$

9   a) Solve the equation. $\frac{x + 4}{3} = \frac{3 - x}{2}$
        First multiply both sides by 6.

    b) Solve the equation. $\frac{x - 4}{2} = \frac{1 - x}{5} + 2$
        First multiply both sides by 10.

10 Solve these equations.

    a) $19e - 5 = 71$ b) $2e + 21 = 5e - 3$ c) $2(k + 5) = 50$

    d) $4(n - 1) + 5 = 41$ e) $3(n + 1) = 42$ f) $2(k - 2) = 5(3 + k) - 5$

    g) $\frac{2c}{5} = 7$ h) $\frac{3}{n + 1} = 2$ i) $\frac{e}{8} + 1 = 3$

1   Problems can often be solved by writing and
    solving an equation.
    In the problem we decide what quantity we need
    to find, and use a letter (eg. x) to represent its value.
    Then we solve the equation.

    Example: Look at the Candles Problem.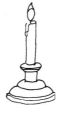
    We need to find the number of candles in a box.
    So, let x stand for the number of candles in a box.
    Then there are $26x + 3$ candles altogether.
    We know that there are 315 candles altogether.
    So $26x + 3 = 315$.

> **Candles Problem**
> 315 candles fit into 26 boxes,
> with 3 candles left over.
> How many candles fit in a box?

   a) Solve the equation yourself.
   b) Check that your value of x fits the original
      problem.

2 a) Write an equation for this problem. ▶
      Use n for the number of candles in a box.
   b) Solve your equation.
   c) Check that your solution fits the problem.

> 179 candles fit into 23 boxes, with
> room left for another 5 candles.
> How many candles fit in a box?

3 a) Copy and complete the equation for
      this problem. Use m for the original
      number of mushrooms in each pile.
      $6(\ldots + \ldots) = \ldots$
   b) Solve the equation.
   c) Check that your solution fits the problem.

> Alan makes 6 equal piles of mushrooms
> for the barbecue.
> He adds another 2 mushrooms to each pile.
> Altogether, this makes 42 mushrooms.
> How many mushrooms were there in each
> pile before 2 more were added?

4 a) Solve the problem by writing
      an equation. Your equation
      should involve brackets.
      Use p for the original lengths
      of the poles.
   b) Check that your solution fits
      the problem.

> Sunita has 7 equal wooden poles.
> She cuts 8 cm from each and arranges them
> to make a heptagon (7-sided figure) with
> perimeter 91 cm.
> How many cm long were the original poles?

5 a) Copy and complete the equation for the
      rectangle problem.
      l cm stands for the length of the rectangle.
      $l + l + (l - 3) + \ldots = \ldots$
   b) Solve the equation.
   c) Check that your solution fits the problem.

> A rectangle has a perimeter of 96 cm.
> Its width is 3 cm less than its length.
> Find the length.

6   Solve these problems by first writing an equation.

a)
> A rectangle with
> perimeter 72 cm
> is half as wide
> as it is long.
> Find the width
> of the rectangle.

b)
> A pentagon with perimeter 66 cm has
> a set of two equal sides and a set of
> three equal sides.
> The two equal sides are both 2 cm
> longer than the other three sides.
> How long are the sides of the pentagon?

7   Solve these problems by first writing an equation.

a)
> A box contains 3 large bolts and
> 2 small bolts.
> The mass of a large bolt is 26 g
> more than the mass of a small bolt.
> The total mass is 270 g.
> What is the mass of a small bolt?

b)
> $\angle DBC = 3 \times \angle ABE$.
> $\angle DBE = 4 \times \angle ABE$.
> Find the
> size of
> $\angle ABE$.

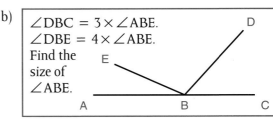

8   Read the egg problem. ▶
Suppose x eggs fit in a box.
a) What does the expression $25x + 90$ tell you?
b) What does the expression $32x + 6$ tell you?
c) Use the expressions in a) and b) to write an
    equation for the problem.
d) Solve your equation. Check that
    the solution satisfies the problem.

> Don is packing eggs.
> When he has filled 25 boxes,
> there are 90 eggs left to pack.
> When he has filled 32 boxes,
> there are 6 eggs left to pack.
> How many eggs fit in a box?

9   Read the garden path problem. ▶
Suppose the length of each slab is l m.
a) What does the expression $8l + 6$
    tell you?
b) Write another expression for the
    length of the path.
c) Use the expressions in a) and b) to
    write an equation for the problem.
d) Solve your equation. Check that
    the solution satisfies the problem.

> Misha is laying a line of
> square slabs to make a
> garden path.
> When she has laid 8 slabs
> she still has 6 m to go.
> When she has laid 13 slabs,
> she has 2 m to go.
> How long is each slab?

10 a) Write an equation for this problem. ▶
        Choose your own letter and say
        what it stands for.
    b) Solve your equation. Check that
        the solution satisfies the problem.

> Carla is buying some tulips.
> If she buys 4 she will have £2.75 left.
> If she buys 9 she will have 40p left.
> How much does each tulip cost?

44

11 For each of the problems A, B, C and D
    a) write an equation, explaining the meaning of any letter that you use
    b) solve the equation
    c) check that the solution fits the problem.

A   Angie and Kate are 3 years old.
    They are sitting on the kitchen floor,
    building towers from cubes.
    Angie's tower is 21 cubes tall; its top
    is 13 cm below the top of the table.
    Kate's tower is 32 cubes tall; its top
    is 20 cm above the top of the table.
    How tall is each cube?

B   51 people travel to a hotel in 9 taxis.
    Altogether there are 3 empty seats.
    How many passengers does a full
    taxi carry?

C   Year 3 at Endle Primary School goes
    on an outing in 3 identical coaches.
    There are 13 spare seats altogether.
    Two full coaches return early, leaving
    31 children for the third coach.
    How many seats does each coach have?

D   The picture shows 3 paper clips and
    a pencil. How long is each paper clip?

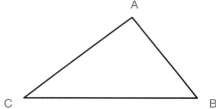

12 The angles of any triangle sum to 180°.
    In the triangle, ∠ABC is 10° larger than ∠ACB.
    ∠CAB is 40° larger than ∠ABC.
    a) Write down an equation whose solution gives
       the size of ∠ACB.
       Explain the meaning of any letters that you use.
    b) Find the size of each angle of the triangle.

13 For each problem A and B
    a) write an equation
    b) solve the equation
    c) check that the solution fits the problem.

A   I think of a number.
    I add 3 to the number, then
    double the result.
    My final result is 22.
    What is my starting number?

B   I think of a number.
    I subtract 5 from the number,
    then multiply the result by 3.
    I get my starting number.
    What is my starting number?

14 The rectangle is 3 cm wide.
    It is 1 cm longer than the square.
    It has the same perimeter as the square.
    a) Use t for the length of side of the square.
       Write down an equation involving t.
    b) Find the length of the rectangle.

1   Compare the two sets of numbers. ▶
    To get the numbers in set B from
    those in set A we multiply by 4.

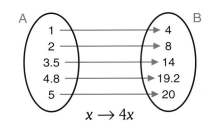

    The numbers in set A could be the
    lengths of sides of squares.
    The numbers in set B could be the
    perimeters of squares.
    We say that the numbers in set A are
    mapped onto the numbers in set B.
    We call the relationship between them
    a 'times 4' mapping.

    Using x for any number in set A,
    we write $x \rightarrow 4x$.

    a) The mapping $x \rightarrow 4x$ maps 2 onto 8.
        Onto which number does it map
        (i) 3   (ii) 12   (iii) 5.5?
    b) Which number does $x \rightarrow 4x$ map onto
        (i) 20   (ii) 56   (iii) 8.4?

2   The diagram represents the mapping
    $x \rightarrow x + 2$, ie the 'add 2' mapping.
    It maps 3 onto 5.
    a) Onto which number does it map
        (i) 7   (ii) 19   (iii) 7.8?
    b) Which number is mapped onto
        (i) 28   (ii) 56   (iii) 9.6?

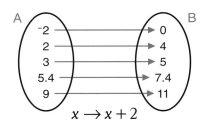

3   The diagram represents the mapping

    $x \rightarrow \dfrac{x}{5}$, ie the 'divide by 5' mapping.

    It maps 10 onto 2 and 30 onto 6.
    a) Onto which number does it map
        (i) 35   (ii) 0.5   (iii) 50?
    b) Which number is mapped onto
        (i) 7   (ii) 12   (iii) 1.1?

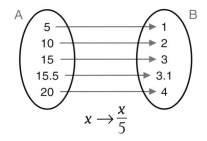

4   The diagram represents the mapping $x \rightarrow 12 - x$,
    ie the 'subtract from 12' mapping.
    It maps 2 onto 10 and 15 onto ⁻3 $(12 - 15 = {}^{-}3)$.
    a) Onto which number does it map
        (i) 5   (ii) 13   (iii) 30?
    b) Which number is mapped onto
        (i) 6   (ii) 0   (iii) ⁻9?

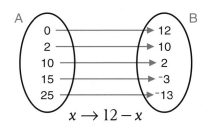

5   $x \rightarrow x - 7$ maps 9 onto 2. ▶
    We say that 2 is the *image* of 9.

Subtract 7

Find the image of 4 for each of these mappings.

a) $x \rightarrow x + 9$ b) $x \rightarrow 3x$ c) $x \rightarrow \dfrac{x}{2}$

d) $x \rightarrow 10 - x$ e) $x \rightarrow \dfrac{12}{x}$ f) $x \rightarrow 2x - 1$

6   a) For the mapping $x \rightarrow 3x$, the image of $^-2$ is $^-6$.
       Write down the image of
       A: $^-1$ B: $^-4$ C: $^-9$.

◀ $3 \times ^-2 = ^-2 + ^-2 + ^-2 = ^-6$

   b) For the mapping $x \rightarrow 2 - 3x$, the image of $^-4$ is 14.
      Find the image of
      A: $^-1$ B: $^-5$ C: $^-9$.

◀ $3x$ is $3 \times ^-4$, which is $^-12$.
So $2 - 3x$ is $2 - ^-12$ which is 14.

7   a) Line diagram A represents the
       mapping $x \rightarrow 3 - x$.
       Draw a line diagram to represent
       $x \rightarrow 2 - x$.
       Show values of x from 2 to $^-2$.
    b) Line diagram B represents the
       mapping $x \rightarrow \dfrac{10}{x}$.
       Draw a line diagram to represent
       $x \rightarrow \dfrac{12}{x}$.
       Show values of x from 1 to 5.

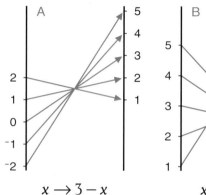

$x \rightarrow 3 - x$

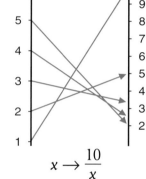

$x \rightarrow \dfrac{10}{x}$

8   Line diagrams A - E are for the same range of values of x.
    Match each one with one of the mappings in the list.

            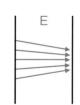

Mappings

$x \rightarrow x + 2$

$x \rightarrow 2x$

$x \rightarrow x - 2$

$x \rightarrow \dfrac{x}{2}$

$x \rightarrow 2 - x$

9   Line diagrams A - E are for the same range of values of x.
    Match each one with one of the mappings in the list.

   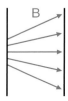   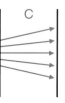   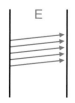

Mappings

$x \rightarrow x + 1$

$x \rightarrow x + 3$

$x \rightarrow x$

$x \rightarrow 2x$

$x \rightarrow 3x$

10 $x \to 2x+1$ is the 'multiply
    by 2 then add 1' mapping.

$$x \to 2x \to 2x+1$$

It combines the
$x \to 2x$
and the
$x \to x+1$
mappings, in that order.
The diagram shows how
it does this. ▶

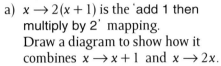

$x \to 2x+1$

a) $x \to 2(x+1)$ is the 'add 1 then
    multiply by 2' mapping.
    Draw a diagram to show how it
    combines $x \to x+1$ and $x \to 2x$.
    Show values of x from $^-1$ to 2.
b) Describe these mappings in words (eg. 'multiply by 4 then subtract 3').
    A: $x \to 3x+1$ B: $x \to 2x-1$ C: $x \to 3(x-1)$
c) For each mapping in part b) list the two mappings which are combined
    (eg $x \to 4x-3$ combines $x \to 4x$ and $x \to x-3$).

11 $x \to 2x+1$ can be
    shown in this single
    mapping diagram. ▶
    Draw a single mapping
    diagram for the mappings
    in part b) of Q 10.
    Show values of x from
    $^-1$ to 2.

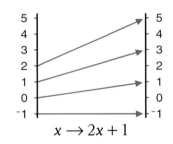

$x \to 2x+1$

12 a) Copy and
       complete
       the two
       tables of
       values.

x	$^-3$	$^-2$	$^-1$	0	1	2	3
$2x-3$	$^-9$						3

$x \to 2x-3$

   b) Draw a
       diagram for
       each mapping.

x	$^-3$	$^-2$	$^-1$	0	1	2	3
$2(x-3)$	$^-12$						0

$x \to 2(x-3)$

13 There is one whole number value of x between $x=0$
    and $x=10$, for which the mappings $x \to 2x-1$ and
    $x \to x+3$ have the same image value.
    What value of x is this, and what is the image value?

14 Find the image of (i) $x=8$ (ii) $x=^-8$, for each mapping.

    a) $x \to \dfrac{x}{2}+3$ b) $x \to \dfrac{x+3}{2}$

Special mappings
This is the 'subtract from 6'
mapping: $x \to 6-x$.
This is the 'Divide into 6'
mapping: $x \to \dfrac{6}{x}$

Describe these mappings in
words:

A: $x \to \dfrac{6}{6-x}$ B: $x \to 6 - \dfrac{6}{x}$.
●●●●●●●●●●●●●●●●●●●●●●●●●●●●●●●

48

1   Look at the mapping diagram. ▶
    It shows $x \rightarrow x + 3$ followed by $x \rightarrow x - 3$.
    The result is $x \rightarrow x$.
    $x \rightarrow x - 3$ undoes what $x \rightarrow x + 3$ does.
    We say that $x \rightarrow x - 3$ is the **inverse**
    of $x \rightarrow x + 3$.

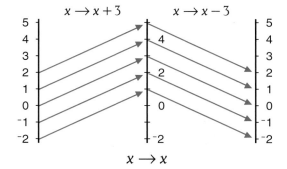

    a) Redraw the diagram to show $x \rightarrow x - 3$
        followed by $x \rightarrow x + 3$.
    b) What is the inverse of $x \rightarrow x - 3$?

2   Write down the inverse of each mapping.
    a) $x \rightarrow x - 2$ b) $x \rightarrow x + 4$ c) $x \rightarrow x - 7$

3   Look at the mapping diagram.
    It shows that $x \rightarrow \dfrac{x}{3}$ is the
    inverse of $x \rightarrow 3x$.

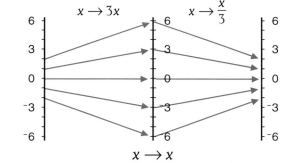

    a) Redraw the diagram to show
        $x \rightarrow \dfrac{x}{3}$ followed by $x \rightarrow 3x$.
    b) What is the inverse of $x \rightarrow \dfrac{x}{3}$?

4   Write down the inverse of each mapping.
    a) $x \rightarrow 4x$ b) $x \rightarrow \dfrac{x}{5}$ c) $x \rightarrow 0.5x$

5   Look at diagram A. ▶
    It shows that $x \rightarrow 3x - 1$ is the '$\times 3$ then -1'
    mapping.
    Look at diagram B. ▶
    It shows that to get back to where we started
    we use the '$+1$ then $\div 3$' mapping.

    So the inverse of $x \rightarrow 3x - 1$ is $x \rightarrow \dfrac{x + 1}{3}$.

$$A \quad x \xrightarrow{\times 3} 3x \xrightarrow{-1} 3x - 1$$

$$B \quad x \xleftarrow{\div 3} 3x \xleftarrow{+1} 3x - 1$$

    a) For the mapping $x \rightarrow 3x - 1$, the image of 12 is 35.
        What is the image of 15?

$$12 \xrightarrow{\times 3} 36 \xrightarrow{-1} 35$$

    b) For the mapping $x \rightarrow \dfrac{x + 1}{3}$, the image of 35 is 12.
        What is the image of 44?

$$35 \xrightarrow{+1} 36 \xrightarrow{\div 3} 12$$

    c) The image of the number k using the mapping $x \rightarrow 3x - 1$, is 20.
        Use the inverse mapping to find k.

6   Look at the table.
    It shows the effect of the mapping
    $x \rightarrow 2x + 5$ on the numbers 3, 4 and 10.
    Write down the inverse of the mapping.
    Make sure that it takes 11, 13 and 25
    back to 3, 4 and 10.

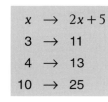

7   Think about the mapping $x \rightarrow \dfrac{x}{3} + 7$.

    It divides any number by 3, then adds 7 to the result.

    The diagram shows the effect of the mapping on the

    number 12, and the effect of the inverse mapping. ▶

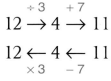

    a) Write the two single mappings $(x \rightarrow \ldots, \ x \rightarrow \ldots)$
        which combine to make $x \rightarrow \dfrac{x}{3} + 7$.
    b) Write the inverse of each of the mappings in part a).
    c) Write down the two mappings which combine to
        produce the inverse of $x \rightarrow \dfrac{x}{3} + 7$.
    d) Write down the inverse, $x \rightarrow \ldots$, of $x \rightarrow \dfrac{x}{3} + 7$.

8   Look at the diagram.
    Use it to help you write
    the inverse mapping of
    $x \rightarrow 3x - 5$.

$$\overset{\times 3}{} \qquad \overset{-5}{}$$
$$10 \rightarrow 30 \rightarrow 25$$
$$10 \leftarrow 30 \leftarrow 25$$
$$\underset{\div 3}{} \qquad \underset{+5}{}$$

9   Think about the mapping $x \rightarrow 8(x - 1)$.
    It subtracts 1 from any number then multiplies the
    result by 8.
    a) Describe the inverse mapping in the same way.
    b) Write the inverse mapping in the form $x \rightarrow \ldots$

10 a) Write down the two mappings, $x \rightarrow \ldots, \ x \rightarrow \ldots$,
        which combine to give the mapping $x \rightarrow 4x + 1$.
    b) Write down the two mappings, $x \rightarrow \ldots, \ x \rightarrow \ldots$,
        which combine to give the inverse of the mapping
        $x \rightarrow 4x + 1$.
    c) Write down the inverse of the mapping $x \rightarrow 4x + 1$.

11 Find the inverse of each mapping.
    a) $x \rightarrow 5x + 9$ b) $x \rightarrow 9(x + 5)$ c) $x \rightarrow \dfrac{x}{5} + 9$ d) $x \rightarrow \dfrac{x + 9}{5}$

Self-inverses
a) Find the image of 2, 3
and 5 for the mapping
$x \rightarrow 6 - x$.
b) Find the image of 4, 3
and 1 for the mapping
$x \rightarrow 6 - x$.
c) Look at your results in
parts a) and b).
The inverse of the
mapping 'subtract from 6'
is 'subtract from 6'!
Find another mapping
which is its own inverse.
d) Is the mapping $x \rightarrow \dfrac{12}{x}$
its own inverse? Explain
your answer.
●●●●●●●●●●●●●●●●●●●●●●●●●●●●

50

1   Look at diagram A and diagram B. ▶
    They both represent the mapping
    $x \rightarrow x + 1$.
    Diagram B is a **graph** of the mapping.

    The two broken lines shows how
    $x = 2$ and its image are connected on
    the graph.
    The dot on these lines is the point $(2, 3)$.

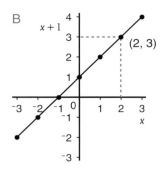

a) The table shows the effect of
    the mapping $x \rightarrow x + 2$ for
    $x = {}^{-}3, {}^{-}2, {}^{-}1, 0, 1, 2$.
    Copy and complete the table.
b) *Use squared paper.*
    Copy the axes and draw
    the graph of $x \rightarrow x + 2$.
c) Copy the axes again.
    Draw the graph of the mapping
    $x \rightarrow x - 1$ for ${}^{-}2 \leq x \leq 3$
    (ie for values of x from ${}^{-}2$ to 3).

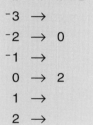

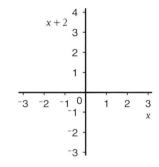

2   Look at the mappings A, B and C.
    A: $x \rightarrow x$ B: $x \rightarrow x - 2$ C: $x \rightarrow 2 - x$
    For each mapping
    a) make out a table of values like that in
        Q1 a), for $x = {}^{-}3, {}^{-}2, {}^{-}1, 0, 1, 2, 3$
    b) draw the graph of the mapping.

Curved graphs
a) Draw a mapping diagram for
   $x \rightarrow x^2$, for $x = 0, 1, 2, 3, 4$.
b) Draw a graph of the mapping
   for $0 \leq x \leq 4$.
c) Draw a mapping diagram for
   $x \rightarrow \dfrac{12}{x}$, for $x = 1, 2, 3, 4$.
d) Draw a graph of the mapping
   for $1 \leq x \leq 4$.
•••••••••••••••••••••••••••••••••••••••

3   Look at graphs P, Q and R.
    Graph P represents the mapping $x \rightarrow 2x$
    for ${}^{-}3 \leq x \leq 4$.

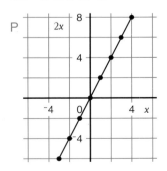

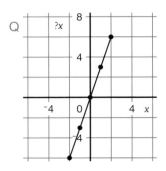

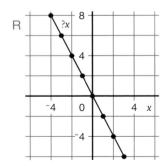

a) Make out a table of values for graph Q.
b) Write down the mapping represented by graph Q.
c) Make out a table of values for graph R.
d) Write down the mapping represented by graph R.

51

4   Look at graphs P, Q and R.
    Graph P represents the mapping $x \rightarrow x + 2$.

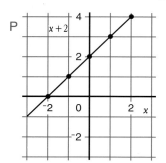 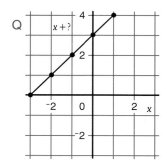 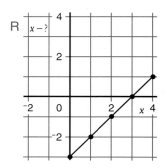

a) Make out a table of values for graph Q.
b) Write down the mapping represented by graph Q.
c) Make out a table of values for graph R.
d) Write down the mapping represented by graph R.

5   Look at graphs P, Q and R.
    Graph P represents the mapping $x \rightarrow 4 - x$.

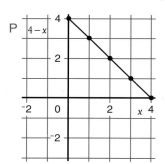 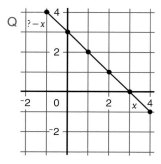 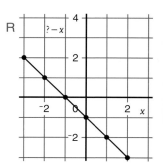

a) Make out a table of values for graph Q.
b) Write down the mapping represented by graph Q.
c) Make out a table of values for graph R.
d) Write down the mapping represented by graph R.

6   The graphs P, Q, R and S are all drawn on the same pair of axes.

    They are for the mappings $x \rightarrow x - 5$, $x \rightarrow 5x$, $x \rightarrow \dfrac{x}{5}$, $x \rightarrow x + 5$.

    Match each mapping with its graph.

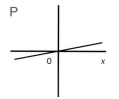 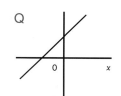 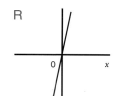 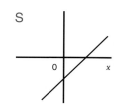

7   Think of the graphs of the three mappings $x \rightarrow x$,
    $x \rightarrow 3x$ and $x \rightarrow 6x$.
    You can draw them if you wish.
    a) Which graph passes through the point $(3, 9)$?
    b) Which graph passes through the point $(^-3, ^-3)$?
    c) Which graph passes through the point $(^-3, ^-18)$?
    d) Write down the coordinates of a point which lies
       on all three graphs.
    e) Which graph is steepest?
    f) Which graph slopes least?

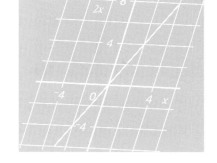

8   Think of the graphs of the three mappings $x \rightarrow ^-x$,
    $x \rightarrow ^-3x$ and $x \rightarrow ^-6x$.
    You can draw them if you wish.
    a) Which graph passes through the point $(3, ^-9)$?
    b) Which graph passes through the point $(3, ^-3)$?
    c) Which graph passes through the point $(^-3, 18)$?
    d) Write down the coordinates of a point which lies
       on all three graphs.
    e) Which graph is steepest?
    f) Which graph slopes least?

9   Look at the mappings A - D.
    Their graphs are straight lines,
    but they have something else
    in common.
    What is it?

    A: $x \rightarrow 3x + 1$
    B: $x \rightarrow 3x + 5$
    C: $x \rightarrow 3x - 4$
    D: $x \rightarrow 3x - 7$

10 Look at the mappings A - C.
    For each mapping
    a) make out a table of values, for
       $x = ^-3, ^-2, ^-1, 0, 1, 2, 3$.
    b) draw the graph of the mapping.

    A: $x \rightarrow 4x$
    B: $x \rightarrow 4(x + 1)$
    C: $x \rightarrow 4x + 1$

11 The graphs P, Q, R and S are all drawn on the same pair of axes.
    They are for the mappings $x \rightarrow 2x + 3$, $x \rightarrow 2(x + 3)$, $x \rightarrow 3x$, $x \rightarrow 3x - 3$.
    Match each mapping with its graph.

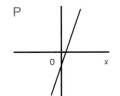
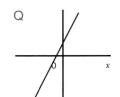
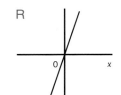
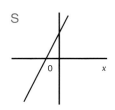

Ma3
Shape, Space and Measures

LD1: Recognise and use common 2-D representations of 3-D objects.
LD2: Know and use the properties of quadrilaterals in classifying different types of quadrilateral.
LD3: Solve problems using angle and symmetry properties of polygons and properties of intersecting and parallel lines, and explain these properties.
LD4: Devise instructions for a computer to generate and transform shapes and paths.
LD5: Understand and use appropriate formulae for finding circumferences and areas of circles, areas of plane rectilinear figures and volumes of cuboids when solving problems.
LD6: Enlarge shapes by a positive whole-number scale factor.

LD1, PoS1: ISOMETRIC DRAWINGS

You need 1 cm dotted isometric paper and/or dotted squared paper for the questions in this exercise.

1   Look at the drawing. ▶
It shows a 3-D (three dimensional) view of a tower made from two cubes. It is drawn on 1 cm dotted **isometric** paper.

Draw the tower laid on its side.

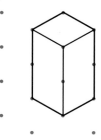

◀ Make sure you have your isometric paper like this, not like this.

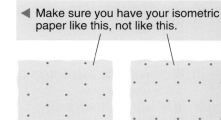

2   This shape is made from 4 cubes.
The grey cube is removed.
Draw the shape that is left.

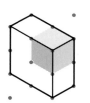

In an isometric drawing, edges which are parallel in real life are shown parallel.
In a perspective drawing, parallel lines are drawn tending towards each other like this:

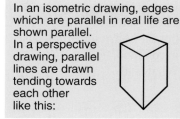
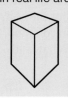

3   In this drawing you can see all of the cubes used to make the shape.
Re-do the drawing. Only draw lines that show edges of the shape.

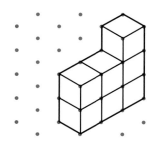

4   This shape is made of 4 cubes.
Lauren adds another cube.
Draw what the shape looks like if she places the cube on
a) square A   b) square B.

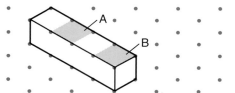

54

5   Aysha, Ben, Carol and Dan are
    looking at the L shape. ▶
    Drawing P shows Aysha's view.

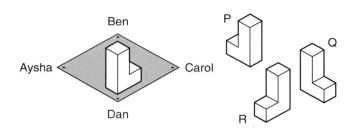

    Whose view does
    a) drawing Q show
    b) drawing R show?

6   Look at the two
    drawings of a
    2 cm cube. ▶
    Pam has used
    1 cm dotted
    isometric paper.
    Paul has used
    1 cm dotted
    squared paper.

    Look at the
    C and the
    L shape.
    a) Draw the
       C shape
       using Paul's
       method.
    b) Draw the
       L shape
       using Pam's
       method.

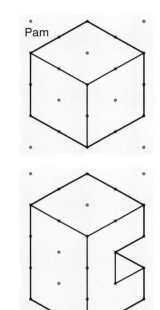

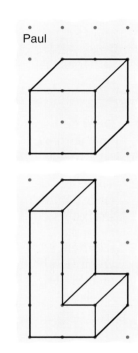

7   It is often important
    to show the hidden
    edges of a shape.
    We do this using
    broken lines. ▶

    a) Draw a cube of any size
       using 1 cm squared paper.
       Use broken lines to show
       the hidden edges.
    b) Sketch a cylinder standing
       on a circular face.
       Use a broken line to show
       the hidden edge.

8   Make an isometric drawing of a solid
    letter H (use broken lines for hidden edges).

In perspective

This is a **perspective** drawing of a cube. Parallel
lines meet at the **vanishing points** P and Q.

a. Make a larger version of the drawing (draw
P and Q about 20 cm apart; make the edge AB
about 3 cm long).

b. Imagine *sliding* the cube to the left, so that
edge AB goes to KL.

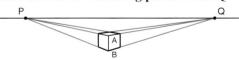

Make a perspective drawing of the cube in its
new position.

c. Draw the cube in other positions.

●●●

You need 1 cm dotted squared paper for the questions in this exercise.

1 Look at the letter L .

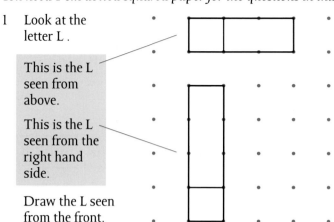

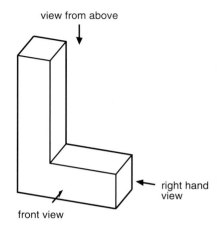

view from above

This is the L seen from above.

This is the L seen from the right hand side.

right hand view

front view

Draw the L seen from the front.

2 The letter C is made from six 1 cm cubes. Draw the C seen from
   a) the front
   b) the right
   c) above.

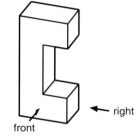

right

front

3 a) This is the front view ▶ of shape A. It is called the **front elevation**.

   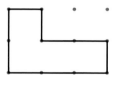

   Shape B is made of 7 cubes. Draw its front elevation.

   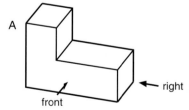

   A

   right

   front

   b) This is shape A seen ▶ from the right hand side. It is called the **right elevation**.

   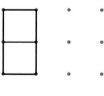

   Draw the right elevation of shape B.

   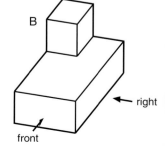

   B

   right

   c) This is shape A seen ▶ from above. It is called the **plan**.

   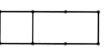

   Draw the plan of shape B.

   front

56

4 Look at shape A.
This is its front elevation. ▶
The broken line shows a
hidden edge.

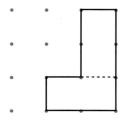
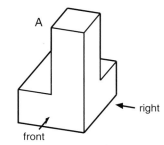

a) Draw the right elevation.
Show the hidden edge
with a broken line.
b) Draw the left elevation.

5 Look at shape A.
Look at views P, Q,
R and S.
Which is
a) the left elevation
b) the right elevation
c) the plan ?

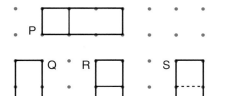
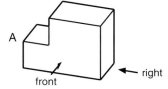

6 *Use isometric paper.*
Look at the shape.
a) Draw a different shape
which has the same
front elevation
b) Draw a different shape
which has the same
plan.

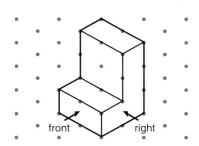

7 Look at the drawings.
They show the plan and front elevation of three cuboids.
Draw the right elevation of each cuboid.

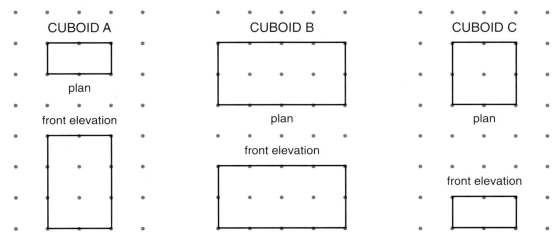

CUBOID A

plan

front elevation

CUBOID B

plan

front elevation

CUBOID C

plan

front elevation

8 Look at the solids, and at the views P - Y.
a) For each solid, decide which view shows the front elevation. Make a list like this:
cube: view P
cylinder: view …
b) Decide which view shows the plan of each solid. Make a list.

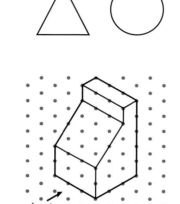

9 The drawing shows a toy cash register. The cash register has a 3 cm by 3 cm square base.
Draw
a) the front elevation
b) the right elevation
c) the plan.

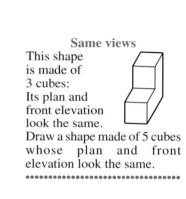

Same views
This shape is made of 3 cubes: Its plan and front elevation look the same.
Draw a shape made of 5 cubes whose plan and front elevation look the same.

10 Look at the table of elevations and plans. Each solid is made from four 1 cm cubes. Draw the missing elevations and plans.

		object A	object B	object C	object D
front					
right					
plan					

11 The shed is 4 ft wide and 8 ft long.
It is 7 ft high in the middle.
The side panels are 5 ft high.
Draw a plan, front elelvation and right elevation of the shed.
Use a scale of 1 cm to1 ft.

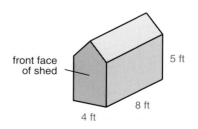

front face of shed

5 ft

8 ft

4 ft

58

1   This shape has 4 straight sides. ▶
    It is called a **quadrilateral**.
    'Quadri' means 'four'.
    'Lateral' means 'side'.
    So 'quadrilateral' means 'four sides'.

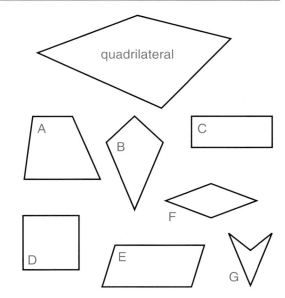

    Shapes A - G are special kinds of quadrilateral.
    Shape A is special because it has a pair of
    parallel sides.
    List the letters of all of the shapes that have
    a) two pairs of parallel sides
    b) four right angles
    c) four equal sides
    d) two pairs of equal sides
       (but not *four* equal sides)
    e) two pairs of equal angles
       (but not *four* equal angles).

2   These are the names of the special quadrilaterals
    in Question 1. ▶

    a) All quadrilaterals which have *two pairs
       of parallel sides* are *parallelograms*.

       A square is a special type of parallelogram.
       Name the two other shapes which are special
       types of parallelogram.

    b) All quadrilaterals which have *four right
       angles* are *rectangles*.

       Name the shape which is a special rectangle.

    c) All quadrilaterals which have *four equal
       sides* are *rhombuses*.

       Name the shape which is a special rhombus.

    d) All quadrilaterals which have *at least one
       pair of parallel sides* are *trapeziums*.

       Name the four shapes which are special trapeziums.

    e) All quadrilaterals with *a line of symmetry
       along a diagonal* are *kites*.

       Name the two shapes which are special kites.

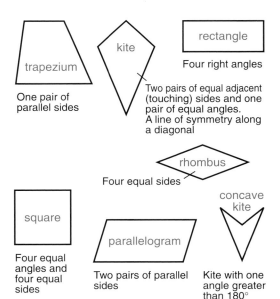

Framed!
This is a wire
framework of
a pyramid:
Explain
why the
black wires do not
make a quadrilateral.
••••••••••••••••••••••••••••

3   *Use dotted squared paper.*
    Copy the drawing three times.
    Complete the shape so that it is
    a) a square
    b) a kite (but not a square)
    c) a trapezium (but not a square).

4   *Use dotted squared paper.*
    Copy the drawing three times.
    Complete the shape so that it is
    a) a parallelogram
    b) a trapezium (but not a parallelogram)
    c) a different trapezium (but not a parallelogram).

5   Think of making quadrilaterals by joining
    some of the points A - G.
    ABCG is a square.
    Name
    a) a parallelogram (but not a square)
    b) another parallelogram
    c) a kite (but not a square)
    d) a trapezium (but not a parallelogram).

6   Look at the statements A - F.
    Statements A, B and C are
    true for all parallelograms.
    a) Which of the statements
        are true
        (i)   for all rectangles
        (ii) for all rhombuses?
    b) For which special kind of
        quadrilateral are all the
        statements true?

A   Both pairs of opposite sides
    are parallel
B   Both pairs of opposite angles
    are equal
C   Both pairs of opposite sides
    are equal
D   Two pairs of adjacent sides
    are equal
E   All four sides are equal
F   All four angles are equal

7   Look at the shapes. ▶
    The square has 4 lines of symmetry,
    and rotational symmetry of order 4.

    List the shapes which have
    a) exactly two lines of symmetry
    b) rotational symmetry of order 2
    c) no lines of symmetry
    d) no rotational symmetry
    e) exactly one line of symmetry.

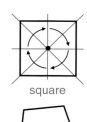

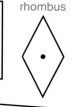

60

1   This is a half turn.      These two angles   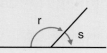   We say that r and s are
    A half turn is 180°.   make a half turn.   **angles on a straight line**.
                                                                                              Angles on a straight line
                                                                                              add up to 180°.

   a) If ∠r is 120°, how many degrees is ∠s ?
   b) If ∠s is 72°, how many degrees is ∠r ?

2   Look at the
    diagrams.
    Write down
    the size of
    angles a, b
    and c.

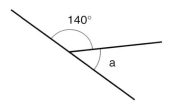 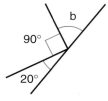 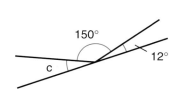

3   This is a full turn.   These three angles   We say that r, s and t are
    A full turn is 360°.   make a full turn.   **angles at a point**.
                                                                                              Angles at a point add up
                                                                                              to 360°.

   a) If ∠r is 35° and ∠s is 245°, how many degrees is ∠t ?
   b) If ∠s is 210° and ∠t is 75°, how many degrees is ∠r ?

4   Look at the
    diagrams.
    Write down
    the size of
    angles a, b
    and c.

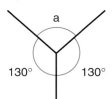 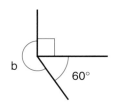 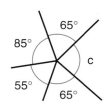

5   The diagram shows two ▶
    straight lines which cross.
    Angles a and c are equal.
    They are called **vertically
    opposite angles**.

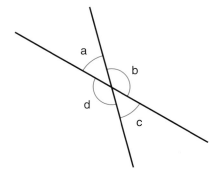

   a) Name the other pair of
    vertically opposite angles.
   b) If ∠a is 50°, how many
    degrees are angles b, c and d ?

Get the angle
Angle p is twice the
size of angle q.
Angles q and r are
the same size.
How many degrees
is angle r if the three
angles are
a. angles on a
straight line
b. angles at a point?

●●●●●●●●●●●●●●●●●●●●●●

6   Look at the diagram.
    APQB is a straight line.
    a) Explain why EPF is *not* a straight line.
    b) Explain why JQK *is* a straight line.
    c) Write down the size of ∠APF.
    d) Write down the size of ∠BQK.

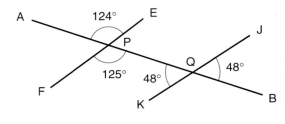

7   The diagram shows three straight lines. ▶
    AB and CD are parallel.
    This means that they cut line EF at the
    same angle.
    So, for example, ∠AXE = ∠CYE.

    ◀ We use
    arrow heads
    to show that
    AB and CD
    are parallel.
    We write
    AB // CD.

    a) Name another pair
       of equal angles.
    b) Name another pair.

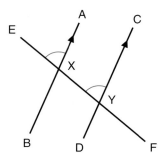

8   Look at the diagram.
    PQ // RS and ∠a = 70°.
    Write down the size
    of angles b, c, d, e, f,
    g and h.

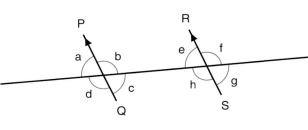

9   Look at the diagrams. ▶
    Angles a and b are called
    corresponding angles.
    Corresponding angles are
    the same size.

    Angles c and d are called
    alternate angles.
    Alternate angles are the
    same size.

    Angles e and f are called
    interior angles.

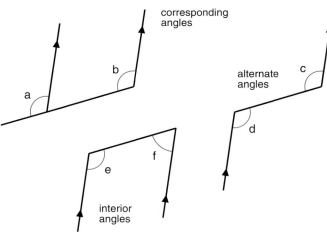

    a) Write down the corresponding
       angle to
       (i) r   (ii) s   (iii) t   (iv) u.

    b) Write down the alternate angle to
       (i) s   (ii) t.

    c) Write down the interior angle to
       (i) s   (ii) t.

    d) Write down three angle equal to
       (i) s   (ii) t.

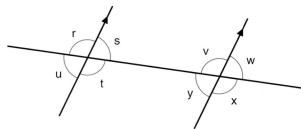

10 Look at the diagram.
   a) Which angle is equal to ∠v?
   b) How many degrees is ∠u + ∠g?
   c) Explain why the interior angles u and v add up to 180°.

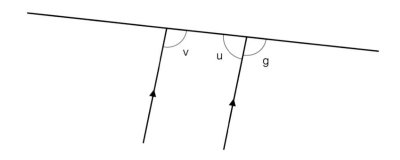

11 All the lines in the diagram are straight.
   ∠ABF is 60° because ∠ABF and ∠BCG are corresponding angles.
   Explain why
   a) ∠BFG is 100°
   b) ∠JFG is 80°
   c) ∠PKL is 110°.

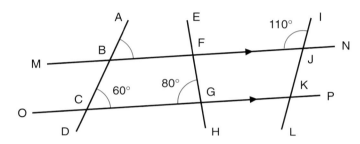

12 All the lines in the diagram are straight.
   a) Which line is parallel to AB? Explain why.
   b) Which line is parallel to CD? Explain why.

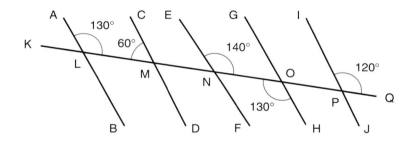

13 Look at the parallelogram ABCD.
   u and v are *opposite angles* of the parallelogram.
   a) Explain why u and v must be equal. (You should mention angle w.)
   b) If angles u and v are 70°, what is the size of the other two angles of the parallelogram?

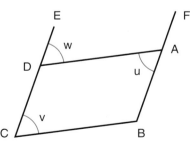

14 Look at the diagram.
   ABCD, CBEF and DCFG are parallelograms.
   Find the size of ∠BEF.

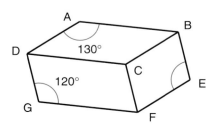

Mmmm
Look at the M shape. Explain why AB is parallel to ED.

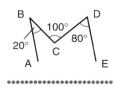

63

1 a) Look at triangle ABC.
       Explain why the sum of its angles
       is 180°.
   b) Look at triangle DEF.
       Do you think its angle sum is 180°,
       less than 180°, or more than 180° ?
       Explain your choice.
   c) Look at triangle GHI.
       Do you think its angle sum is 180°,
       less than 180°, or more than 180° ?
       Explain your choice.

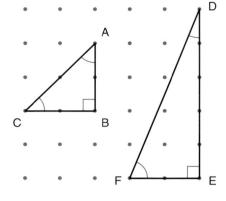

2 Look at triangles
   X, Y and Z.
   The sizes of two
   angles in each
   triangle are given.

   For each triangle,
   a) find the size of
       angles a, b, and
       c, in that order
   b) find the angle sum.

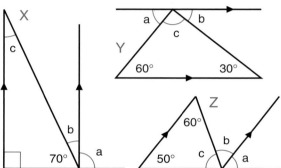

3 Margie draws a triangle.
   She calls the angles a, b and c.
   She draws a line parallel to one of the sides.
   She marks the angles d and e.

   a) Which angle is equal to angle a ? Give a reason.
   b) Which angle is equal to angle c ? Give a reason.
   c) The sum of angles d, b and e is 180°. Explain why.
   d) Think of your answers to parts a), b) and c).
       Explain why the sum of angles a, b and c is also 180°.

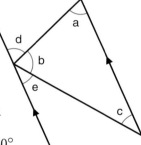

4 Question 3 shows that **the angle sum of any triangle is 180°.**

   Use this to explain why each angle of an equilateral triangle is 60°.

5 Look at the quadrilateral.
   It has been divided into two triangles.
   a) What is the sum of angles a, b and c ?
   b) What is the sum of angles r, s and t ?
   c) Think of your answers to parts a) and b).
       Explain why the sum of the angles of the
       quadrilateral is 360°.

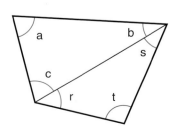

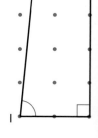

6   Use the method in Question 5.
    Find the sum of the angles of
    a) the pentagon
    b) the hexagon.

pentagon

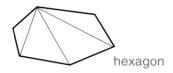

hexagon

7   Look at the octagons (8-sided polygons).
    They have been divided into 6 triangles.
    a) Draw you own octagon.
       Divide it into 6 triangles.
    b) Copy then complete: The angle sum
       of any octagon is ☐ × 180° = ☐°.

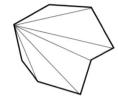

8   Use your result in
    Question 7 to explain
    why the angles of a
    regular octagon are 135°.

135°

◀ A **regular** polygon has sides all the same
   length and angles all the same size.

9   Find the angle sum
    of a polygon with
    a) 10 sides
    b) 12 sides
    c) 22 sides.

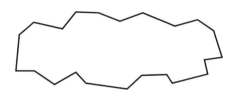

Side search
Each angle of a
regular polygon is
160°.
How many sides
does it have?
●●●●●●●●●●●●●●●●●●●●●●●●

10 X, Y and Z are
    isosceles triangles.
    In each triangle the
    size of one angle is
    given.
    Write down the size
    of the other two angles
    in each triangle.

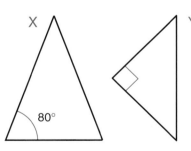

X

80°

Y

Z

120°

◀ An isosceles triangle
   has two equal sides
   and two equal angles.

11 Look at the regular pentagon.
    It has been divided into 5 congruent triangles.
    a) Explain why ∠AOB is 72°.
    b) Explain why ∠ABO is 54°.
    c) Explain why each angle of the regular
       pentagon (eg, ∠EAB) is 108°.

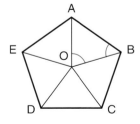

A

E

O

B

D

C

12 Find the size of each angle of
    a) a regular hexagon
    b) a regular 10 sided poygon
    c) a regular 20 sided polygon.

◀ Use the method
   of Q 11.

360-gon
A regular polygon
has 360 sides.
What is the size of
its angles?
●●●●●●●●●●●●●●●●●●●●●●

13 A regular polygon has rotational symmetry
of order 12.
Calculate the size of each of its angles.

14 The trapezium has
a line of symmetry.
Find the size of
a) angle p
b) angle q
c) angle r.

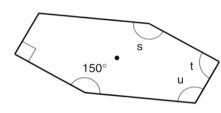

Exterior angles
This drawing shows the
exterior angles of a
regular pentagon:

15 The hexagon has rotational
symmetry of order 2.
Find the size of
a) angle s
b) angle t
c) angle u.

a. How many degrees is
each exterior angle?
b. How many degrees is
each exterior angle of
i. a regular hexagon
ii. a regular 10-gon ?

16 a) Find the sizes of the other three
angles of rhombus ABCD.
Give reasons for each of your
answers.
b) Look at the kite EFGH.
What is the size of angle g if
angle f is
(i) 90° (ii) 110° (iii) 130° ?

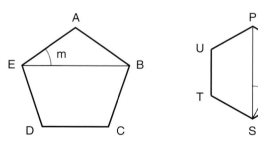

17 a) ABCDE is a regular pentagon.
Find the size of angle m.
(Use your result in Question 11
to help you.)
b) PQRSTU is a regular hexagon.
Find the size of
(i) angle k
(ii) angle n.

18 Kamlesh makes two copies of the isosceles
triangle from cardboard.
She fits them together to make a quadrilateral.
Sketch the quadrilateral and mark on it the size
of its angles, if Kamlesh makes
a) a rhombus
b) a parallelogram (but not a rhombus)
c) a kite (but not a rhombus).

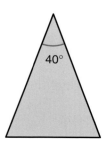

66

You will need a computer for question parts marked (*), to check or investigate instructions.

1   A turtle is at point A. ▶
    It faces up the page.
    These instructions take
    it from A to B to C.

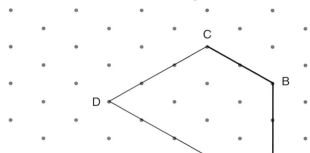

FORWARD 300
LEFT 60
FORWARD 200

a) The turtle has arrived at C.
    Write an instruction that turns it to face D.
b) Write the instruction that now takes the turtle to D.
c) Which of these instructions will now turn the turtle
    to face A ?
    LEFT 60 or LEFT 120 or LEFT 300
d) Write the instruction that now takes the turtle to A.
e)* Use a computer. Check the whole set of instructions.

2   A turtle traces the path ABCDE. ▶
    At B it turns through ∠b.
    At C it turns through ∠c.
    At D it turns through ∠d.

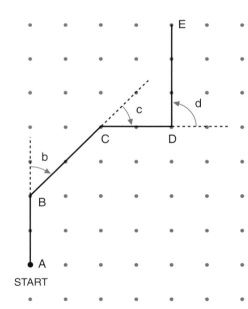

a) Write down the size of angles b, c and d.
b) Copy and complete these instructions for
    the path ABCDE.

FD 200   ◀ FD is short for FORWARD
RT ___   RT is short for RIGHT
FD 283   LT is short for LEFT
RT ___
FD ___
LT ___
FD ___

c)* Use a computer. Check the instructions.

3   A turtle traces the path PQRST.
    At Q it turns through an angle of 90°.
    a) Sketch the path.
        Mark the angle the turtle turns
        through at R and S.
    b) Write a set of instructions for
        the path.

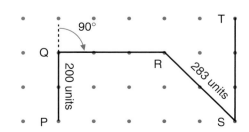

4 ABC is an equilateral triangle.
   A turtle is at A and faces up the page.
   a)* Use a computer. Check that these instructions
       produce the path ABCA.
       FD 300   RT 120   FD 300   RT 120   FD 300
   b) Write a sixth instruction so that the turtle faces
       up the page again.

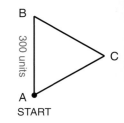

5 A turtle traces these shapes.
   It is placed on the point
   marked START, and faces
   up the page each time.
   Write instructions that
   produce
   a) the square ABCD
   b) the square EFGH
   c) the rectangle IJKL
   d) the rectangle MNOP.

6 Path PQR is a reflection of path ABC.
   These instructions produce ABC.
   LT 20   FD 100   LT 60   FD 200
   Write instructions for path PQR.

7 These instructions take a turtle along the
   path ABCD.
   FD 50   RT 80   FD 200   LT 30   FD 100
   This instruction turns the turtle round.
   LT 180
   Write instructions that now take the turtle
   back along the path DCBA.

8 a)* Use a computer. Check that
       these instructions produce
       the parallelogram ABCD.
       FD 300
       RT 50
       FD 200
       RT 130
       FD 300
       RT 50
       FD 200
   b) Write instructions that produce
       the parallelogram JKLM.
   c) Write instructions that produce
       the parallelogram PQRS.

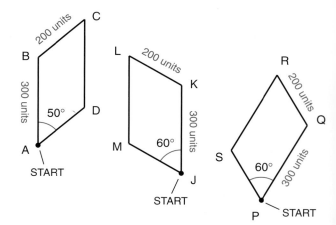

68

9 The turtle is facing North.
In which direction is it facing after these instructions?
a) FD 100 RT 90 FD 100 RT 90 FD 100
b) FD 100 LT 90 FD 100 RT 90 FD 100
c) FD 100 RT 45 FD 100 RT 45 FD 100
d) FD 100 RT 45 FD 100 LT 135 FD 100

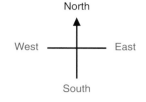

10 a)*Use a computer. Complete these instructions
   to produce the 'house' (find the length of the
   base by trial and improvement).
   FD 200 LT 30 FD 200 LT 60 FD 400 …
   b) Rewrite the instructions to add a chimney to
   the house.

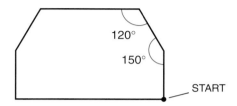

11 These instructions produce the ? shape.
FD 50 RT 90 FD 50 LT 90 FD 100
LT 90 FD 100 LT 90 FD 50
   a) Write instructions that produce a 'stretched'
   ? shape that is
      (i) twice as tall but just as wide
      (ii) twice as wide but just as tall.
   b)*Use a computer to check your instructions.

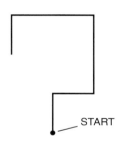

12 a) Write instructions
   that produce a path
   like
      (i) zig zag A
      (ii) zig zag B.
   b)*Use a computer
   to check your
   instructions.

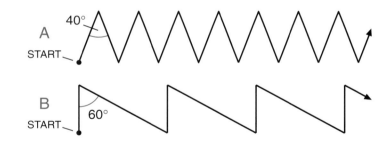

13 a)*Use a computer to check that these
   instructions produce a regular pentagon.
   REPEAT 5 (FD 20 RT 72)
   b) Write similar instructions that produce
      (i)   a regular hexagon
      (ii) a regular octagon
      (iii) a regular 20 sided polygon.

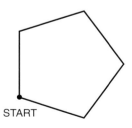

Italicise
Write instructions
that produce a
slanting version of
the ? shape in
Q11.

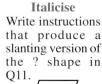

14 a)*Use a computer to check that these instructions give
   a hexagon.
   REPEAT 3 (FD 100 RT 40 FD 50 RT 80)
   b) Modify the instructions to produce another hexagon.
   Write down the instructions.

1   The distance ▶
    around a circle
    is called the
    circumference.

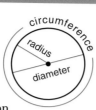

Petra draws this design on
1 cm squared paper. ▶

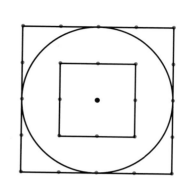

a) What is the diameter of the circle?
b) What is its radius?
c) Write down the perimeter of
    (i)   the smaller square
    (ii) the larger square.
d) Which of these do you think is the
    best estimate for the circumference
    of Petra's circle?
    4×4 cm 3×4 cm 2×4 cm

2   Look at the drawing.
    AB is a piece of string that just fits around the circle.
    a) Measure the diameter (d mm) of the circle.
    b) Measure AB to find the circumference (C mm) of the circle.
    c) Which of these do you think is the best estimate?
        $C = 2 \times d$ $C = 3 \times d$ $C = 4 \times d$

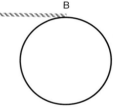

3   It turns out that for *any* size circle, the ▶
    circumference (C) is about 3 times bigger
    than the diameter (d):
    C = a number (about 3) $\times d$.

    The number is called π ('pi') and we write
    $C = \pi d$.

    π is about $3\frac{1}{7}$ or about 3.142.

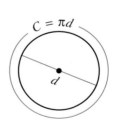

◀ π is a strange number.
Although it has a fixed
value, it cannot be
written exactly as a
fraction or decimal.
If you wanted to write
it exactly as a decimal,
you would have to go
on writing for ever.
π is 3.1415926536,
correct to 10 decimal
places.

Look at circle W.
Its circumference is about 3.1×8 cm, or 24.8 cm.
Estimate the circumferences of circles X, Y and Z.
Use $\pi = 3.1$ for each estimate.

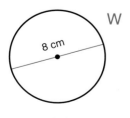

W

8 cm

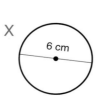

X

6 cm

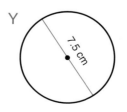

Y

7.5 cm

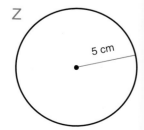

Z

5 cm

4   Use a calculator with a π key.
    To find the circumference of this ▶
    circle, press
    $\boxed{C}\ \boxed{\pi}\ \boxed{\times}\ \boxed{9}\ \boxed{=}$.

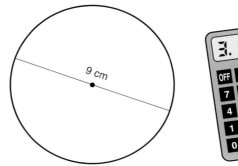

    Use your calculator.
    Calculate the circumference
    correct to
    a) the nearest cm
    b) the nearest mm.

5   Use your calculator. Find the circumference of each circle correct to 2 DP.
    a) Diameter 8.8 cm   b) Diameter 17 m   c) Radius 9 cm

6   Carol bends the wire into a circle. ▶
    She wants to calculate the diameter.
    The circumference is 24 cm, so
    $\pi \times$ Diameter $= 24$.
    So Diameter $= 24 \div \pi$.

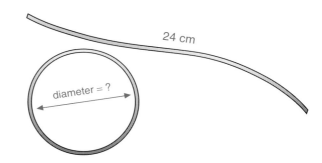

    Use your calculator.
    Find the diameter of the circle correct
    to the nearest cm.

7   a) Find the diameter of each circle correct to the nearest mm.
        (i)   Circumference $= 57$ cm
        (ii) Circumference $= 108$ cm
    b) Find the *radius* of each circle correct to the nearest mm.
        (First find the diameter, then divide by 2.)
        (i)   Circumference $= 72$ cm
        (ii) Circumference $= 56$ cm

8   The diameter (d) of a circle
    is twice the radius (r). ▶
    The circumference (C) is
    $\pi \times d$, or $\pi \times 2 \times r$.

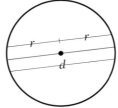

    We write $C = 2\pi r$.

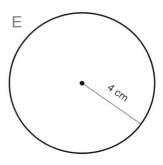

    a) To find the circumference of circle E, we press these keys:
        $\boxed{C}\ \boxed{2}\ \boxed{\times}\ \boxed{\pi}\ \boxed{\times}\ \boxed{4}\ \boxed{=}$.
        Find the circumference correct to the nearest mm.
    b) Find C, correct to 1 DP, for each of these values of r.
        (i) 15   (ii) 9.8   (iii) 28.6

9 Petra draws this design on 1 cm squared paper. ▶
  a) The area of the blue region is 3×3 cm^2 = 9 cm^2.
     How many times larger is the area of
     (i) square EFGH   (ii) square PQRS?
  b) Which of these do you think is the best
     estimate for the area (A cm^2) of the circle?
     $A = 2 \times 3 \times 3$
     $A = 3 \times 3 \times 3$
     $A = 4 \times 3 \times 3$

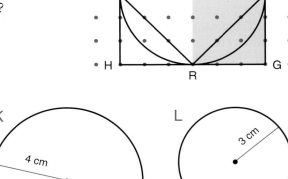

10 The area (A) of any circle turns ▶
   out to be $\pi \times$ radius $\times$ radius.
   So $A = \pi \times r \times r = \pi r^2$.

   The area of circle K is
   A cm$^2 = \pi \times 4^2$ cm$^2 = 16\pi$ cm^2,
   which is 50 cm^2 correct to the
   nearest 1 cm^2.

   Use your calculator. Find the area,
   correct to the nearest 1 cm^2, of
   a) circle L
   b) circle M.

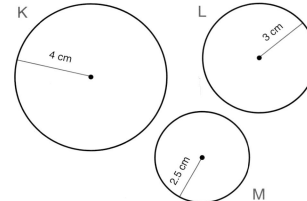

Radius search
A circle has an
area of 150 cm^2.
Find its radius, to
the nearest cm.
●●●●●●●●●●●●●●●●●●●●●

11 Use the formula $A = \pi r^2$.
   Calculate the area of each circle correct to the nearest 1 cm^2.
   a) radius 5 cm   b) radius 10 cm   c) radius 7 cm

12 a) Calculate the area of
      each shape correct to
      the nearest 1 cm^2.
   b) Calculate the perimeter
      of each shape correct to
      the nearest mm.

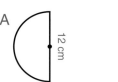

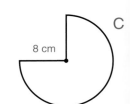

13 This is a large metal washer. ▶
   a) Calculate the area, correct
      to 2 DP, of
      (i) a 5 cm diameter circle
      (ii) an 8 cm diameter circle.
   b) Use your results in part a).
      Find the area of the face
      of the washer, correct to
      the nearest 1 cm^2.

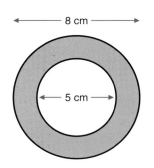

Out of order
Ken says "8 cm − 5 cm
is 3 cm, so the area of
the face of the washer
in Q 13 is $\pi \times 3^2$ cm^2."
Do you agree? Why?
●●●●●●●●●●●●●●●●●●●●●●●

.1　Look at rectangle A. ▶
It has 6 whole 1 cm squares and 0.3 of a 1 cm square.
So its area is 6.3 cm².

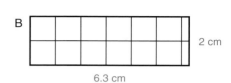

A

6.3 cm

1 cm

a) Explain why the area of rectangle B is 12.6 cm².
b) A third rectangle is as long as rectangle A, but
is 3 cm wide.
What is its area?
c) Find the area of a rectangle which is 6.3 cm long
and 8 cm wide.

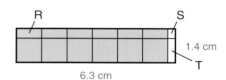

B

6.3 cm

2 cm

2　Look at the 6.3 cm × 1.4 cm rectangle. ▶
The area of the grey part is 6 cm² (6 × 1 cm²).
The area of the part marked R is 0.4 cm² because
it is 0.4 of a whole 1 cm square.
So the area of the blue part is 2.4 cm² (6 × 0.4 cm²).
The part marked S is 0.3 of a 0.4 cm² part.
So its area is 0.12 cm² (0.3 × 0.4 cm²).
The area of the part T is 0.3 cm² (0.3 × 1 cm²).

R　　　　　　　　　S

6.3 cm

1.4 cm

T

a) Use the information above to find the area of the
whole rectangle.

b) Notice that the area of the rectangle is
6 × (1 cm² + 0.4 cm²) + 0.3 × (1 cm² + 0.4 cm²),
which is (6 + 0.3) × 1.4 cm², which is 6.3 × 1.4 cm².

Check that this gives the result you found in part a).

3　Look at the rectangle. ▶
Q1 and Q2 show that we find its area (A cm²) by
multiplying the length (a cm) by the width (b cm):

$A = ab$.　　◀ ab means a × b.

A cm²

b cm

a cm

a) Use the formula. Find the area of a rectangle measuring
　(i) 3.2 cm by 5 cm　　　(ii) 9.5 cm by 8.5 cm.
b) Use the formula. Find A when
　(i) a is 2 and b is 15　　(ii) a is 9 and b is 6.

4　The rectangle is 5.5 cm long
and 3.5 cm wide. ▶
Find its area by
a) counting whole, half and
quarter squares
b) using the formula $A = ab$.

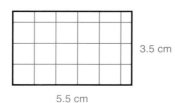

3.5 cm

5.5 cm

Side by side
The area of a rectangle
is 2.5 cm².
a. Write down a pair of
possible lengths for its
sides.
b. Write down another
pair of possible lengths.
●●●●●●●●●●●●●●●●●●●●●●●●●●●●

73

5 Divide these shapes into rectangles. Use the formula $A = ab$. Find the area of each shape.

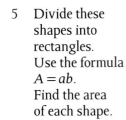

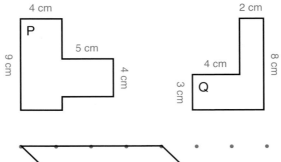

Square challenge
This square has an area of 2 cm².

Use a calculator. Find the length of the square's sides, correct to the nearest mm.

6 Look at the parallelogram. Find its area by counting 1 cm squares and half 1 cm squares.

7 Look at the diagram. ▶ It shows how a parallelogram can be changed into a rectangle.

   a) Explain why the parallelogram and rectangle have the same area.
   b) Find the area of the parallelogram.

   5 cm

8 a) *Use dotted square paper.* Make a sketch to show how parallelogram X can be changed into a 6 cm by 4 cm rectangle.
   b) Parallelogram Y can be changed into a rectangle. Write down the length and width of the rectangle.
   c) Write down the areas of X and Y.

   6 cm

9 Parallelogram ABCD has a **base** of 9 cm, and a **height** of 7 cm. ▶
   Its area is the same as a 9 cm by 7 cm rectangle.
   So its area is 9×7 cm², which is 63 cm².

   This **formula** gives the area, A cm², of a parallelogram with base b cm and height h cm:
   $A = $ base $\times$ height, or $A = bh$.

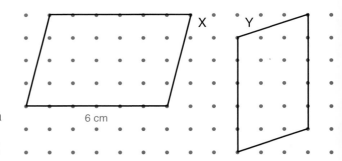

   Use the formula. Find the area of a parallelogram with
   a) base 8 cm and height 4 cm
   b) base 12 cm and height 6.2 cm.

74

10 Calculate the area of each parallelogram.

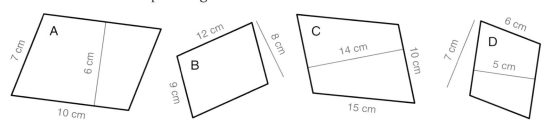

11 The area of the
    parallelogram
    is 12×7 cm^2,
    which is 84 cm^2.
    What is the area
    of each triangle?

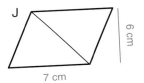

So far apart
The sides of a parallelogram are
4 cm and 5 cm long.
The 4 cm sides are 10 cm apart.
How far apart are the 5 cm
sides?
•••••••••••••••••••••••••••••••••••••

12 Find the area of
    a) parallelogram J
    b) each triangle in J
    c) parallelogram K
    d) each triangle in K.

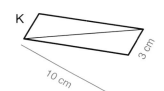

13 Any triangle is half of a parallelogram. ▶
    The area of the parallelogram is base × height, or bh.
    So the area (A) of the triangle is $\frac{1}{2}$(base × height), or $\frac{1}{2}bh$.
    We say: The area of a triangle is half the base times the height.
    We write $A = \frac{1}{2}bh$.

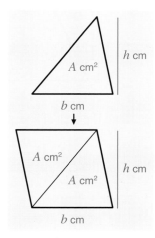

The area of
triangle P is
$\frac{1}{2} \times 8 \times 5$ cm^2,
which is 20 cm^2.
Find the area of
triangles Q - T.

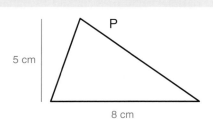

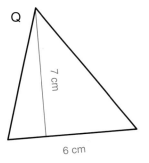

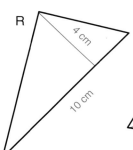

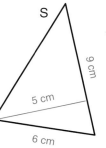

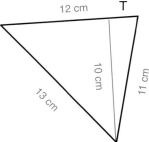

1   Look at the trapezium ABCD. ▶
    It can be divided into two triangles.

    a) Find the area of triangle ACD.
    b) Find the area of triangle ABC.
    c) Use your results in parts a) and b).
        Find the area of the trapezium.

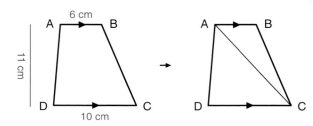

2   Any trapezium can be ▶
    divided into two triangles.
    So the area (A) of the
    trapezium is

    $A = \frac{1}{2}ah + \frac{1}{2}bh$.

    The area of trapezium P
    is $\frac{1}{2}.4.5$ cm^2 + $\frac{1}{2}.8.5$ cm^2,
    which is 10 cm^2 + 20 cm^2,
    which is 30 cm^2.
    Find the areas of
    trapeziums Q, R and S.

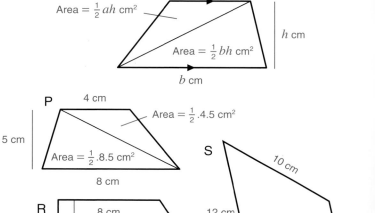

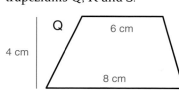

3   Find the area of a trapezium whose parallel sides are 8 cm and 12 cm long, and 7 cm apart.

4   Anil draws a trapezium. ▶
    He cuts it into two parts and makes it into
    a parallelogram.
    The area (A) of the parallelogram is
    base × height, or $(b + a) \times \frac{1}{2}h$.
    So the area (A) of the trapezium is also
    $A = (b + a) \times \frac{1}{2}h$, or $A = \frac{1}{2}(b + a)h$.
    We say: The area of a trapezium is half the
    sum of the two parallel sides times the height.

    The area of trapezium P is $\frac{1}{2}.3.(6 + 8)$ cm^2, which
    is 21 cm^2.
    Use the formula $A = \frac{1}{2}(b + a)h$.
    Find the areas of trapeziums Q, R and S in Question 2.

76

5   Look at the kite ABCD. ▶
    It can be divided into
    two identical triangles.

    The kite is 6 cm wide
    and 10 cm tall.
    What is the area of
    a) each triangle
    b) the kite?

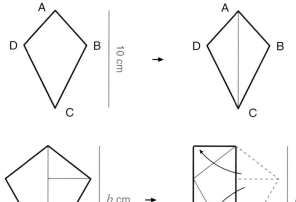

6   Patrick cuts the kite into 3 parts
    and makes a rectangle. ▶

    a) The rectangle is b cm high.
        How wide is it?
    b) The area of the rectangle is
        $\frac{1}{2}a \times b$ cm^2 or $\frac{1}{2}ab$ cm^2.
        What is the area of the kite?

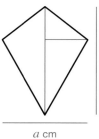

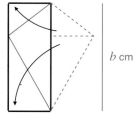

7   In Question 6 we found that the area (A) of a kite is ▶
    $A = \frac{1}{2}ab$.
    We say: The area of a kite is half the product of the
    diagonal lengths.
    (We multiply the diagonal lengths and halve the result.)

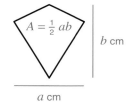

    The area of kite P is $\frac{1}{2}.5.12$ cm^2,
    which is 30 cm^2.
    Use the formula $A = \frac{1}{2}ab$.
    Find the areas of kites Q, R and S.

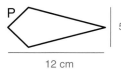

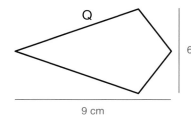
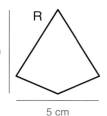

8   These kites and trapeziums are on a 1 cm square grid. Calculate their areas.

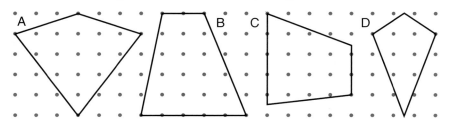

Square kite
A square has
2 cm long
diagonals.
Find its area.
●●●●●●●●●●●●●●●●

1   Ailish is building a tower from 1 cm cubes.
    She builds it on a 3 cm by 5 cm rectangular base.
    a) How many cubes cover the base?
    b) How many cubes does Ailish need altogether
        if the tower is
        (i)   4 cm high
        (ii) 10 cm high
        (iii) 50 cm high ?

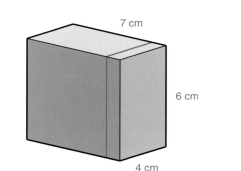

2   Paul cuts the block into 1 cm thick slices.
    The blue lines show the cut marks for the
    first slice.
    a) How many slices does he get?
    b) He cuts the slices into 1 cm cubes.
        How many cubes does he get
        (i) from 1 slice   (ii) altogether?
    c) The volume of each cube is 1 cm³.
        What is the volume of the whole block?

3   Cuboid P is made from 1 cm cubes. ▶
    It stands on a 3 cm by 4 cm base.
    So the number of 1 cm cubes in the
    bottom layer is 3 × 4.
    It is 5 cm high, so there are 5 layers.
    So the total number of 1 cm cubes is
    5 × 3 × 4, which is 60.

    ◀ A cuboid is a solid with
    six, rectangular, faces.

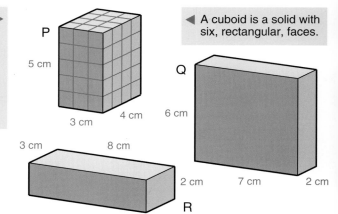

    a) What is the volume of cuboid P ?
    b) How many 1 cm cubes are needed
        to make cuboid Q ?
    c) What is the volume of cuboid Q ?
    d) What is the volume of cuboid R ?

4   The cuboid is made of 1 cm cubes. ▶
    The number of 1 cm cubes in the bottom layer is $a \times b$.
    There are c layers, so the total number of 1 cm cubes is $a \times b \times c$.
    So this **formula** gives the volume (V cm³) of the cuboid:
    $V = a \times b \times c$, or $V = abc$.
    We say: The volume of a cuboid is length × breadth × height.

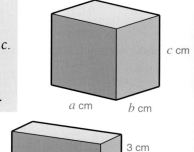

    The volume of this cuboid is $12 \times 4 \times 3$ cm³, which is 144 cm³.
    Use the formula $V = abc$. Find the volume of a cuboid that is
    a) 7 cm high, 2 cm wide, 10 cm deep
    b) 3 cm high, 4 cm wide, 1 cm deep.

5 The cuboid is made of whole cubes and half cubes.
   a) How many whole cubes are there?
   b) How many half cubes are there?
   c) Use your results in parts a) and b). Write down the volume of the cuboid.
   d) Find the volume of the cuboid using the formula $V = abc$.

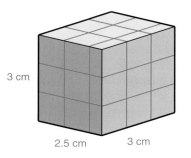

3 cm

2.5 cm   3 cm

Heavy water
The mass of a 1 cm cube of water is 1 g. What is the mass of a 1 m cube of water
a. in g
b. in kg
c. in tonnes ?

6 Find the volume of cuboids A, B and C.

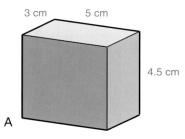

3 cm   5 cm

4.5 cm

A

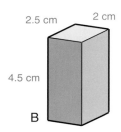

2.5 cm   2 cm

4.5 cm

B

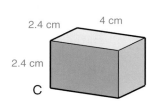

2.4 cm   4 cm

2.4 cm

C

7 Find the volume of
   a) a cuboid with base area 17 cm² and height 4 cm
   b) a cuboid measuring 6 cm by 3.2 cm by 8 cm
   c) a cube with edges 5 cm long.

8 Look at box P. ▶
   The number of 1 cm cubes it can hold is $2 \times 3 \times 5$, which is 30.
   Its **capacity** is 30 cm³.

   What is the capacity of
   a) box Q   b) box R ?

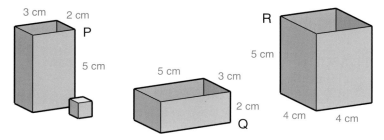

3 cm   2 cm   P

5 cm

R

5 cm

5 cm   3 cm

2 cm

Q

4 cm   4 cm

9 a) 1 cc of water is 1 cubic centimeter of water. How many cc of water can a fish tank measuring 40 cm by 18 cm by 12 cm hold?
   b) 1 litre is 1000 cc. How many litres of water can the fish tank hold?

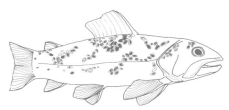

10 a) Barry is making a 10 cm cube from 1 cm cubes. How many 1 cm cubes does he need?
    b) Bob wants to make a 20 cm cube. He tells Barry,
       "I will need twice as many 1 cm cubes as you".
       Use the formula $V = abc$. Show that Bob is wrong.

Small filling
A 50 cc tube of toothpaste comes in a 3.2 cm by 3.5 cm by 13.4 cm box. Roughly what fraction of the box is filled with toothpaste?

1 Look at shapes A and B.
The curved arcs are semicircles.
a) Use $\pi = 3$ to find an estimate
for the perimeter of
(i) shape A   (ii) shape B
b) Use $\pi = 3$ to find an estimate
for the area of
(i) shape A   (ii) shape B.

Perimeter
of a circle
= 2πr.
Area of a
circle = πr².

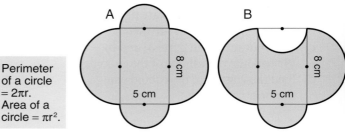

2 Look at shapes A and B.
The curved arcs are quarter circles.
a) Use $\pi = 3.1$ to find an estimate
for the perimeter of
(i) shape A   (ii) shape B
b) Use $\pi = 3.1$ to find an estimate
for the area of
(i) shape A   (ii) shape B.

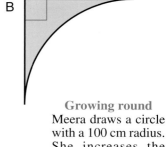

Growing round
Meera draws a circle
with a 100 cm radius.
She increases the
radius by 1 cm.
Use $\pi = 3.1$. Roughly
what is the increase in
a. the circumference
b. the area ?
••••••••••••••••••••••••

3 a) Use use $\pi = 3$
to estimate
the area of
the D shape.
b) Find the area
of the Y shape.

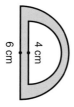
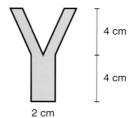

4 ABCD is a parallelogram; AB and DC are 7 cm apart.
a) Find the area of the parallelogram.
b) Find the areas of triangles AED, EBC and CDE.
c) Point E moves 1 cm closer to B, along AB.
The area of one of the triangles stays the same.
Which triangle is it?

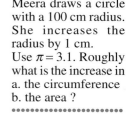

5 The drawing shows two strips of card.
The strips are 4 cm and 6 cm wide.
AB = 8 cm.
a) Find the area of ABCD
b) Find the length of BC.

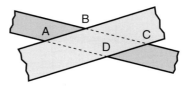

Trapped
A circle with diameter
8 cm just fits inside a
rhombus of sides
12 cm.

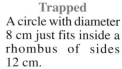

6 Drawings A and B include
the same pair of rectangles.
Explain why the shaded area
in diagram A is greater than
that in diagram B.

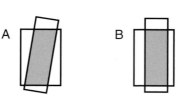

Find the area of the
rhombus.
••••••••••••••••••••••••

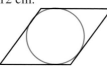

7   Look at the net of the wedge.
    a) Find the area of the slanting face.
    b) Find the total area of the net.
    c) Pam makes two copies of the wedge.
       She sticks them together to make
       a cuboid.
       What is the volume of the cuboid?

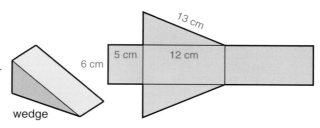

wedge

8   A kite has diagonals 8 cm and 4 cm long.
    a) Make a sketch of the kite.
    b) Find its area.

9   Net ABCDEFGH is for the
    square based pyramid.
    Find
    a) the area of face CDE
    b) the total area of the net.

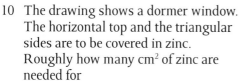

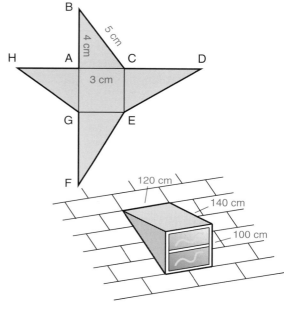

10 The drawing shows a dormer window.
    The horizontal top and the triangular
    sides are to be covered in zinc.
    Roughly how many cm² of zinc are
    needed for
    a) one triangular side
    b) altogether?

11 The drawing shows an empty swimming pool.
    The pool is 9 m wide and 30 m long.
    It is 1 m deep for the first 10 m of its length.
    It drops steadily for the next 10 m, and is
    4 m deep for the last 10 m.
    a) Find the area of the vertical wall A.
    b) When the pool is full, what volume of
       water is there
        (i) in the shallowest part of the pool
        (ii) at the deep end?

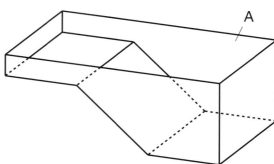

12 Pam is designing an aluminium
    duct for a restaurant's kitchen.
    The drawings show a 3-d view and
    an elevation of the duct.
    Pam wants to know the area of face A.
    a) Sketch face A.
       Divide it into shapes whose area
       you can find.
    b) Find the total area of face A.

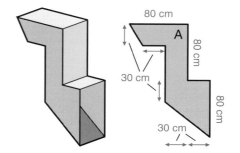

You need 1 cm dotted squared paper for the questions in this exercise.

1   Look at the shapes. ▶
     Shape B is an **enlargement** of shape A.
     All the lengths are twice as long as those
     in shape A.
     All the angles are the same as those in
     shape A.

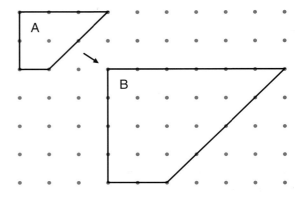

     Draw another enlargement of shape A.
     Make all the lengths
     a) three times as long
     b) four times as long.

2   Look at shape ABCDE. ▶
     Pam uses this method to enlarge it.
     She chooses any point and calls it O.
     She draws a line from O through A to A',
     so that $OA' = 2 \times OA$.
     She does the same for points B, C, D, E.
     This gives a '×2' enlargement.
     O is called the **centre of enlargement**.
     We say the **scale factor (SF)** of the
     enlargement is ×2.

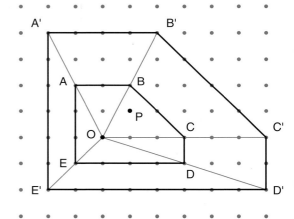

     Copy shape ABCDE and the point P.
     Draw an enlargement of ABCDE with
     scale factor ×3.
     Use P as the centre of enlargement.

3   Look at the shapes.
     JKLM is an enlargement of ABCD.
     a) Which point is the centre of enlargement,
        W, X, Y or Z?
     b) Has the distance of points from the centre
        been *doubled, trebled* or *quadrupled*?
     c) Compare AD and JM.
        Is JM *two, three* or *four* times as long as AD?
     d) Write down the scale factor for the enlargement.

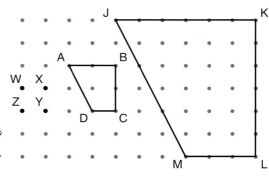

4   a) Copy and
        complete the
        enlargement.
     b) What is the
        scale factor of
        the enlargment?

5 a) Copy the rectangle and enlarge it with scale factor × 4.
       Use A as the centre of enlargement.
   b) Repeat part a) but use (i) B, (ii) C as the centres of
       enlargement.
   c) Write down what you notice about the enlarged rectangles.

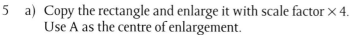

6 Choose a letter in your name.
   a) Enlarge the letter with scale factor × 2 and a centre
       (i) to the left of the letter   (ii) on the letter.
   b) Check that you get the same size letter both times.
       Write down the height of the enlarged letter and
       the original letter.

7 Nisha has tried to enlarge
   triangle ABC.
   a) *One* of the points J, K, L
       is wrong. Which one?
   b) What mistake do you
       think Nisha has made?

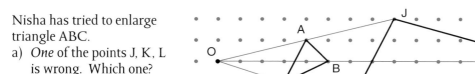

8 Look at the drawing of the enlargement.
   Paul says the scale factor is × 2 because
   OA × 2 = AJ.
   Is Paul correct? If you say 'No', write
   down the correct scale factor.

9 Look at the enlargement of the shape
   ABCD.
   OA = 5 cm, AP = 15 cm, AD = 2 cm.
   Write down
   a) the scale factor for the enlargement
   b) the length of PS.

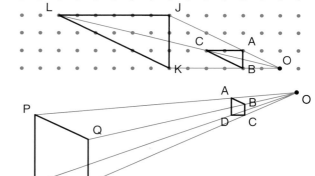

10 A 5 cm by 6 cm rectangle is enlarged.
    Write down its new size, if the scale factor is
    a) × 2   b) × 5   c) × 10   d) × 1.

11 A 4 cm square is enlarged.
    Write down the scale factor if the enlarged
    square has sides of length
    a) 12 cm   b) 20 cm   c) 100 cm   d) 4 cm.

12 Look at the shapes
    JKLM and PQRS.
    Explain why neither
    shape can be an
    enlargement of
    ABCD.

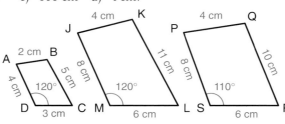

Enlarged circle
Draw a circle with
radius 4 cm. Mark 8
points   on   its
circumference. Call
them A, B, C, …
Choose a centre of
enlargement inside
the circle but *not* at
its centre.
Use a scale factor
× 2. Mark the new
positions of A, B, C,
…   Sketch   the
enlargement of the
whole circle.
Do you think the
enlargement is a
circle? Why?
••••••••••••••••••••••••

Ma4
Handling Data

LD1: Pupils collect and record continuous data, choosing appropriate equal class intervals over a sensible range to create frequency tables.
LD2: They construct and interpret frequency diagrams.
LD3: They construct pie charts.
LD4: Pupils draw conclusions from scatter diagrams, and have a basic understanding of correlation.
LD5: When dealing with a combination of two experiments, pupils identify all the outcomes, using diagrammatic, tabular or other forms of communication.
LD6: In solving problems, they use their knowledge that the total probability of all the mutually exclusive outcomes of an experiment is 1.

LD1, PoS1: FREQUENCY TABLES FOR CONTINUOUS DATA

1 These are the heights, in mm, of 10 tomato seedlings:
29, 21, 19, 28, 36, 17, 22, 15, 24, 32.
The frequency table is for heights (h mm) in these **class intervals**:
$10 \le h < 20$, $20 \le h < 30$, $30 \le h < 40$.
($10 \le h < 20$ means h is equal to or greater than 10, but less than 20.)

Heights of 10 seedlings

Height	Frequency
$10 \le h < 20$	3
$20 \le h < 30$	
$30 \le h < 40$	

a) Copy and complete the frequency table.
b) Make out another freqency table.
Use the intervals $10 \le h < 15$, $15 \le h < 20$, …

2 These are the masses (m grams) of 12 mushrooms:
12, 58, 20, 35, 9, 40, 19, 21, 28, 36, 14, 30.
Pam decides to write the masses in this frequency table. ▶
a) Explain why the 20 g mass goes into the interval $20 \le m < 40$ and not the interval $0 \le m < 20$.
b) Copy then complete the table.
c) Make out another freqency table.
Use the intervals $0 \le m < 10$, $10 \le m < 20$, …

Masses of 12 mushrooms

Mass	Frequency
$0 \le m < 20$	
$20 \le m < 40$	
$40 \le m < 60$	

3 The frequency table is for the lengths (l cm) of 20 goldfish.
a) How many goldfish are
(i) at least 15 cm long
(ii) at least 10 cm long
(iii) less than 15 cm long?
b) One of the goldfish is 5 cm long.
Write down the class interval to which it belongs.
c) Make out another freqency table.
Use the intervals $0 \le l < 10$, $10 \le l < 20$.
d) Explain why it is not possible to change the original table to one with these intervals:
$0 \le l < 4$, $4 \le l < 8$, … , $16 \le l < 20$.

Lengths of 20 goldfish

Length	Frequency
$0 \le l < 5$	2
$5 \le l < 10$	6
$10 \le l < 15$	9
$15 \le l < 20$	3

4   20 people take part in a hopping competition.
    This list gives the best hop (h cm) for each
    person, written in order:
    103, 106, 119, 123, 128, 130, 139, 140,
    142, 146, 151, 154, 154, 159, 160, 160,
    164, 171, 172, 180.
    a) Copy and complete frequency table A.
    b) Copy and complete frequency table B.
    c) The 106 cm hop was Kate's.
        Explain why she might prefer the results to
        be reported in table B rather than table A.
    d) The 164 cm hop was Rubin's.
        Explain why he might prefer the results to
        be reported in table A rather than table B.

A

Distances of 20 best hops

Distance	Frequency
$100 \leq h < 120$	3
$120 \leq h < 140$	
$140 \leq h < 160$	
$160 \leq h < 180$	

B

Distances of 20 best hops

Distance	Frequency
$100 \leq h < 140$	
$140 \leq h < 180$	

5   In a cookery speed test 30 students are each asked to peel
    a 200 g potato.
    These are their times (t seconds), written in order.
    11, 12, 12, 13, 15, 15, 15, 16, 16, 16, 16, 16, 17, 18, 18,
    18, 18, 19, 19, 19, 20, 20, 21, 22, 22, 23, 25, 28, 30, 34.
    The teacher wants to record the times in a frequency table.
    What equal class intervals might she use if she wants to
    a) group the times into five grades (A, B, C, D and E) and
        record how many of each grade there are
    b) give each time a 'Pass' or 'Fail' grade and record how
        many Passes and how many Fails there are?

6   Pavel wants to record the heights (h m) of
    some trees in a frequency table.
    The heights range from a little more than
    11 m to a little less than 30 m.
    Write down a sensible set of class intervals
    which Pavel could use, if he wants
    a) 5 equal class intervals
    b) 4 equal class intervals
    c) 2 equal class intervals.

Frequent birthdays
Find the birthdays of students in your class.
Work out how many full days have passed since the last birthday of each person.
Write the data in a frequency table, with intervals of 40 days (your last interval might be smaller than the others, or you might be able to use equal intervals throughout - it depends upon your data).
Write a paragraph describing something of interest that the distribution shows.
•••••••••••••••••••••••••

7   The frequency table shows the times (t seconds) for 47 people
    to walk across a footbridge.
    All the people walked at their normal speed.
    a) How many people crossed the bridge in less than 32 secs?
    b) How many metres wide do you think the bridge is?
        Explain how you decided.
    c) The ages of the people ranged from 18 years to 89 years.
        In which age range do you think there were more people,
        18 - 25 or 60 - 89? Why?

Times taken to cross bridge

Time	Frequency
$20 \leq t < 24$	1
$24 \leq t < 28$	14
$28 \leq t < 32$	26
$32 \leq t < 36$	5
$36 \leq t < 40$	0
$40 \leq t < 44$	1

1   These are the running times for
    12 tracks on a CD.
    2 min 15 secs   2 min 23 secs
    2 min 35 secs   2 min 43 secs
    2 min 51 secs   2 min 58 secs
    3 min 43 secs   4 min 0 secs
    4 min 10 secs   4 min 43 secs
    5 min 45 secs   7 min 8 secs.

Times of tracks on a CD

Time (t min)	Frequency
$0 \leq t < 2$	0
$2 \leq t < 4$	7
$4 \leq t < 6$	
$6 \leq t < 8$	

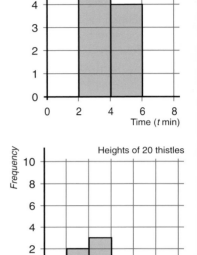

Times of tracks on a CD

    a) Copy and complete the frequency table.

    b) The chart is a **frequency diagram.** ▶
       Notice that the class intervals
       are shown on the horizontal axis.

       Copy and complete the diagram.

2   The frequency table and the
    frequency diagram are for the
    heights (h cm) of 20 thistles.
    a) Copy then complete the
       diagram.
    b) Draw another frequency
       diagram for the data.
       Use these class intervals:
       $10 \leq h < 30$, $30 \leq h < 50$,
       $50 \leq h < 70$.

Heights of 20 thistles

Height	Frequency
$10 \leq h < 20$	1
$20 \leq h < 30$	2
$30 \leq h < 40$	3
$40 \leq h < 50$	9
$50 \leq h < 60$	4
$60 \leq h < 70$	1

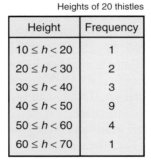

Heights of 20 thistles

3   Vivek has a small apple tree in his garden.
    The frequency diagram shows the masses
    of the apples he picked last year.
    a) How many apples had a mass smaller
       than 150 g?
    b) How many apples did he pick?
    c) Vivek estimates that he picked at least
       2 kg of apples.
       Explain why he must be wrong.

6 apples with
a mass of 50 g
or more, but
less than 100 g.

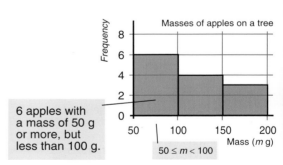

Masses of apples on a tree

4   Lisa had a holiday in Bognor last year.
    Every day she recorded the number of
    hours of sunshine.
    The frequency diagram shows the results.
    a) How many days had at least 4 hours
       of sunshine?
    b) How many days long was Lisa's holiday?
    c) Lisa says that most of the days had less
       than 6 hours of sunshine.
       Can this be correct? Explain why.

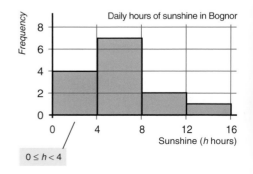

Daily hours of sunshine in Bognor

$0 \leq h < 4$

5 Kirsten digs up two potato
plants.
The frequency diagrams
show the masses (in g) of
the potatoes from each plant.
a) Which plant, A or B,
produced more potatoes?
b) Which plant do you think
produced the larger total
mass of potatoes?
Explain how you decided.

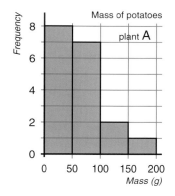

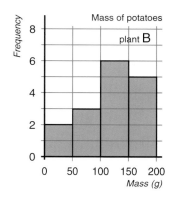

6 The frequency diagrams
show the heights of the
sunflowers in two gardens.
a) Which garden, A or B,
(i) has more sunflowers
(ii) has more sunflowers
160 cm tall or taller?
b) Which garden's sunflowers
do you think are more
uniform in height?
Explain how you decided.

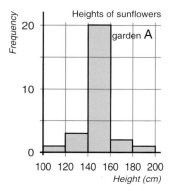

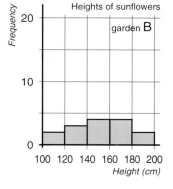

7 Paula works for a bus company.
She answers travel enquiries on
the telephone.
The frequency diagram shows
the times she spent on calls
during one typical hour at work.
Paula names calls that take less
than 2 minutes 'Simple' calls.
She names calls which take 2 or
more minutes 'Complex' calls.
a) Did Paula receive more Simple
calls or more Complex calls
in the hour?
b) Do you think Paula spent more
time altogether on Simple calls
or on Complex calls?
Explain how you decided.
c) Paula works a 7-hour day.
Roughly how many calls do
you think she can answer in
that time?
Explain your answer.

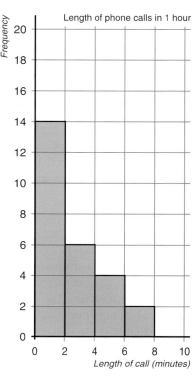

8   The list shows the length (*l* mm) of a selection of leaves collected
    from under two trees.

    Tree A: 12, 23, 35, 40, 49, 54, 62, 63, 69, 71, 71, 78, 79, 80,
             82, 85, 91, 92.

    Tree B: 9, 14, 17, 20, 28, 34, 34, 35, 38, 45, 51, 52, 63, 81.

    a) Use these class intervals:
       $0 \leq l < 20$, $20 \leq l < 40$, $40 \leq l < 60$, $60 \leq l < 80$, $80 \leq l < 100$.
       Draw a frequency diagram for
       (i) Tree A   (ii) Tree B.
    b) Compare your diagrams.
       Do you think the two sets of leaves are from the same type
       of tree? Explain your answer.

9   The list shows the ages (*y* years) of people in a waiting room.

51	2	61	5	11	52	65	65	50	4	25	26
71	21	64	29	58	1	61	4	60	6	49	69
77	42	79	2	66	20	3	70	18	59	72	68

    a) Produce a frequency table for the data.
       Use equal class intervals, starting with $0 \leq y < 10$.
    b) Draw a frequency diagram.
    c) The waiting room is at either at a doctor's surgery or a railway
       station.
       Which do you think is more likely? Why?

10 Petra, Ken and Meera each throw
    15 darts at a circular board, aiming
    for the centre.
    They measure the distance (in cm)
    of each dart from the centre.
    The frequency diagrams show the
    results.
    Petra is the most accurate thrower.
    Ken and Meera are both quite good,
    but Ken is more consistent.
    Match the diagrams with the three
    people.

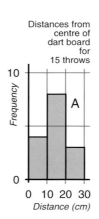

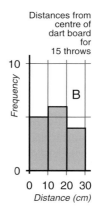

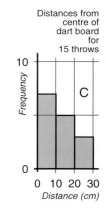

11 The frequency diagram gives the scores
    of students in class 2W in a maths exam.
    a) How many students took the exam?
    b) Estimate how many students scored
       more than half marks.
    c) Students whose marks were more
       than 70% were given an A grade.
       Estimate how many students were
       given an A grade.

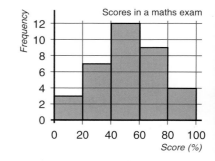

You need a protractor, ruler and compasses.

1 Pam asks twenty 5-year olds which of these drinks
   they like best:
   Cola, Milk, Orange.
   The table shows her results. ▶

Cola	Milk	Orange
4	11	5

She wants to draw a pie chart to show the results.
First she makes a sketch to show the chart. ▶
Then she calculates the angles:

The angle for the whole chart is 360°.
So each child is represented by $360° \div 20 = 18°$.
So the angle for Cola is $4 \times 18° = 72°$.

a) Calculate the angle for Milk.
b) Calculate the angle for Orange.
c) Check that the angles for Cola, Milk and
   Orange add up to 360°.
d) Draw a circle with radius about 4 cm, mark
   the centre, and draw the chart accurately.

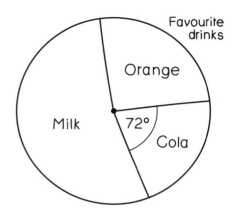

2 Samir records the colours of 40 cars in a car park.
   He sketches a pie chart for his results.

   He calculates the angle for each car:
   $360° \div 40 = 9°$.
   He then calculates the angle for green cars:
   $8 \times 9° = 72°$.

   a) Calculate the angle for
      (i) red cars   (ii) black cars
      (iii) yellow cars   (iv) blue cars.
   b) Check that the five angles add up to 360°.
   c) Draw an accurate pie chart to show the results.

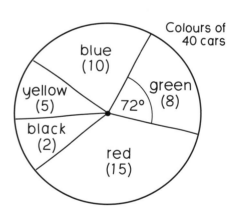

3 60 people are asked which of these
   four sports they like best:
   badminton, netball, tennis, volleyball.
   The pie chart shows the results.
   a) Calculate how many degrees of
      the chart represent one person.
   b) Calculate the angle for
      (i) badminton   (ii) netball
      (iii) tennis   (iv) volleyball.
   c) Check that the angles for the
      four sports add up to 360°.
   d) Draw the pie chart accurately.

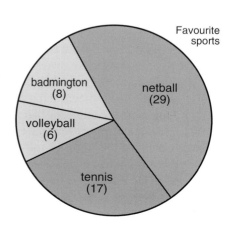

89

4   A jeweller has a stock of 40 bracelets.
    The table shows which metal each is
    made from.
    a) Copy and complete the table.
    b) Draw a pie chart for the information.

	gold	silver	platignum	copper
number	8	24	5	3
pie chart angle	72°			

5   The table shows what fraction of the runners
    in a fun marathon race belong to various age
    groups. ▶
    For example, $\frac{3}{10}$ of the runners are in the
    18 - 25 year old age group.
    So the angle of a pie chart for 18 - 25 year olds
    is $\frac{3}{10}$ of 360°, which is 108°.

Ages of runners in a race

age	fraction	pie chart angle
18 - 25	$\frac{3}{10}$	108°
26 - 40	$\frac{3}{8}$	
41 - 55	$\frac{1}{5}$	
over 55	$\frac{1}{8}$	

   a) Calculate the angle for 26 - 40 year olds.
   b) Calculate the angle for 41 - 55 year olds.
   c) Calculate the angle for over 55 year olds.
   d) Check that the 4 angles sum to 360°.
   e) Draw a pie chart for the information.

6   This is what a national report says about
    river pollution:
    One third of all rivers are severely polluted.
    Two fifths of all rivers are highly polluted.
    The remainder ($\frac{4}{15}$) are acceptable.
    The report includes the pie chart.
    Calculate the angle of the pie chart for
    a) severe pollution
    b) high level pollution
    c) the 'acceptable' sector.

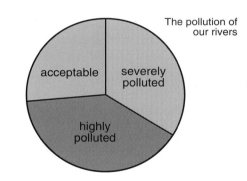

The pollution of
our rivers

7   Ted counted the different types of birds
    in his garden at 8.00 one morning.
    Altogether he saw 18 birds.
    One sixth were blackbirds; one ninth
    were robins; one third were pigeons;
    the remainder were sparrows.
    a) How many were blackbirds?
    b) The pie chart shows Ted's results.
        Calculate the angle for blackbirds.
    c) How many were robins?
    d) Calculate the angle for robins.
    e) How many were pigeons?
    f) Calculate the angle for pigeons.
    g) How many were sparrows?
    h) Calculate the angle for sparrows.

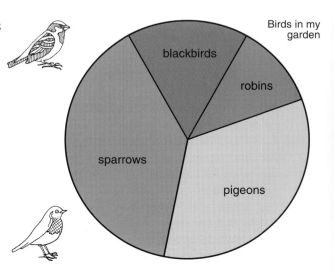

Birds in my
garden

8   Look at the table. ▶
    It shows the ingredients of a bottle of orange
    and lime squash.
    Anil sketches the pie chart for the information.
    To calculate the angle for water, he thinks:
    100 % is 360°.
    75 % is .75 × 360°, which is 270°.

water	75 %
pure orange juice	10 %
pure lime juice	15 %

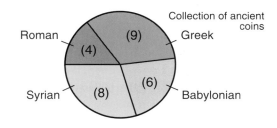
Ingredients of orange & lime squash

    a) Calculate the angle for orange juice.
    b) Calculate the angle for lime juice.

9   In a cookery test all students are given one
    of the grades A, B, C, D and U.
    The table shows the percentage of students
    in one year obtaining each grade.
    The teacher prepares the table ready to draw
    a pie chart.
    Copy and complete the table.

Grades in a cookery test

grade	A	B	C	D	U
percentage	15	23	45	12	5
pie chart angle	54°				

10 Look at the pie chart.
    It shows the numbers of ancient
    coins from different countries in
    a museum display.
    Calculate the angle of a pie chart
    for each country, correct to the
    nearest 0.1°.

Collection of ancient coins

Roman — (4) — (9) — Greek

Syrian — (8) — (6) — Babylonian

11 George draws a pie chart to show the
    proportions of stamps he has from the
    different continents in his collection.
    Altogether George has 480 stamps.
    a) The angle for Europe is 30°.
        How many European stamps are there?
    b) The angle for Asia is 45°.
        How many Asian stamps are there?
    c) 20 % of the stamps are Australasian.
        How many are Australasian?
    d) What is the angle of the pie chart
        for Australasian stamps?

Travel chart
Ask students in your
class where they spent
their last summer
holiday.
Draw a pie chart to
represent your results.
Decide yourself
which categories to
use (eg, holidays
abroad, holidays at
home, …)

12 A necklace is made from 90 beads.
    a) In a pie chart drawn to show the
        number of beads of each colour,
        the angle for red beads is 36°.
        How many of the beads are red?
    b) The angle for green beads is 160°.
        How many of the beads are green?

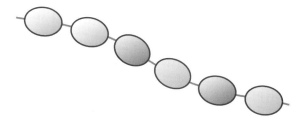

1   24 students were asked to memorise 10 words
     and to write them down 1 hour later.
     The **scatter diagram** shows the ages of
     the students and the number of words
     they remembered. ▶
     For example, the chart shows that the three
     6-year olds remembered 1, 3 and 4 words.

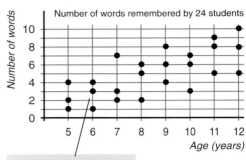

     a) How many words did the three 7-year olds
        remember?
     b) How old were the students who remembered
        8 words?

     The three 6-year olds remembered 1, 3 and 4 words.

2   This is the chart for Question 1 again. ▶
     The broken line suggests a general trend.
     Paula says that it suggests that older
     students tend to remember more words.

     This example supports Paula's statement:
     *There is a 5-year old who remembered 2 words
     and a 6-year old who remembered 3 words.*

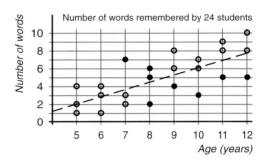

     a) Give another example which supports
        Paula's statement.
     b) Give an example which does *not* support
        the statement.
     c) Choose the 8-year old student who remembered 5 words.
        The hollow dots show the results which support the statement, compared
        to this student. How many are there?
     d) How many results do not support the statement compared   ◀ Ignore the other 8-year olds.
        to this 8-year old?   They neither support nor
                                                                     contradict the statement.
     e) Choose the 10-year old student who remembered 6 words
        (i) How many of the results support the statement compared to this student?
        (ii) How many do not support the statement?
     f) Try some examples of your own.
        For most examples, more results support the statement than do not support it.
        That is why our eye 'sees' a movement from bottom left to top right.

3   The scatter diagram shows the mass
     and length of 30 trout.
     Imagine a dotted line showing the
     general trend.
     a) Meena catches a 2508 g trout.
        Write an estimate for its length.
     b) James catches a 31 cm trout.
        Write down an estimate for its mass.

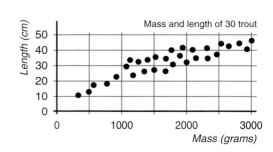

4   Some students were asked to find
    the word 'oxygen' in a dictionary.
    The time taken by each of them
    to find the word was recorded.
    The scatter diagram shows the
    students' ages and their times.
    a) Which of A and B would you
       say is the general trend?
       A: Older students tend to be
          quicker at finding the word.
       B: Older students tend to be
          slower at finding the word.
    b) Choose the 6-year old student who took 40 secs.
       Compared to this student, how many of the results
       (i)   support the statement you chose in part a)
       (ii) do not support the statement you chose in part a) ?

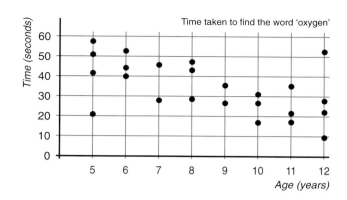

oxygen *n*. an odourless, colourless,
gaseous element; highly reactive
and essential for respiration and
most combustion. Symbol: O;
atomic no: 8; atomic wt: 15.9994.

5   Pam measures the length and width of 14 leaves from a bay tree.

    She draws a scatter diagram.
    a) Which diagram, A, B, C
       or D, is most likely to be
       her diagram?
    b) Explain your choice.

6   Twelve concert goers were asked
    how many CDs they owned with
    music by Mozart and by Brahms.
    The table shows the results.

Number of Mozart CDs	5	14	2	3	20	15	2	20	3	2	8	11
Number of Brahms CDs	3	10	8	2	7	8	5	12	16	1	7	7

    a) Use squared paper.
       Copy the axes and complete
       the scatter diagram.
    b) Which of these do you think
       is true?
       A: More Mozart CDs tends to
          mean more Brahms CDs.
       B: More Mozart CDs tends to
          mean fewer Brahms CDs.
    c) Choose the person who owns
       14 Mozart CDs.
       Compared to this person, how
       many of the results
       (i)   support your choice in part b)
       (ii) do not support your choice ?
    d) Clara owns 10 Mozart CDs.
       Roughly, how many Brahms CDs
       would you expect her to own?

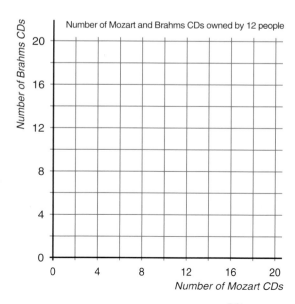

7   The scatter diagram shows the ages and
     heights of 20 beech trees in a small copse.
     The crosses tend to cluster into a line
     from bottom left to top right.
     The pattern shows that older trees tend
     to be taller than younger trees.
     a) Choose the 2-year old tree which is
        1 m tall.
        Compared to this tree, how many trees
        (i)   support the statement that older
              trees are taller than younger trees
        (ii) do not support the statement?

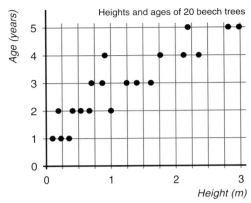

     b) We say that there is a positive relationship, or **positive correlation**,
        between the age of the trees and their heights.
        Height and age tend to increase together.

        Are these positively correlated? Write 'Yes' or 'No'.
        A: Heights and ages of children between 1 year and 10 years old.
        B: Heights and ages of people between 40 and 50 years old.
        C: Ages of cars and their current prices.

8   The scatter diagram shows the ages and
     prices of 20 second hand cars.
     The crosses tend to cluster into a line from
     top left to bottom right.
     The pattern shows that the price tends to
     decrease with age.
     a) Choose the 3-year old car which costs
        £5000.
        Compared to this car, how many cars
        (i)   support the statement that the
              older is the car, the lower is the price
        (ii) do not support the statement?

     b) We say that there is a **negative correlation** between the age and price of the car.
        Price tends to decrease as age increases.

        Write 'negative correlation' or 'positive correlation' for each of these.
        A: The lengths of canal boats and their masses.
        B: The amounts of water in some pans and the times they take to boil.
        C: The ages of people between 50 and 80 and the distances they can walk in 1 hour.

9   Look at the scatter diagrams.
     Which one shows
     a) a positive correlation
     b) a negative correlation
     c) no clear correlation?

10 For each situation A, B, C, D and E say whether you think there is
   • a positive correlation
   • a negative correlation, or
   • no correlation.
   A: The number of rooms in houses in a road and the house number.
   B: The number of rooms in houses in a road and the number of bathrooms.
   C: Marks in a Physics test and marks in a Chemistry test.
   D: The number of cigarettes smoked each day and time to run 100 m.

11 A Science test and a French test are both
   graded Credit, Pass or Fail.
   The table shows the results for 20 students
   who took both tests.
   a) How many students failed both tests?
   b) How many student failed Science but
      did not fail French?
   c) How many students were given a Credit
      grade on both tests?
   d) Do you think the results show a positive
      correlation, a negative correlation or no
      correlation?
      Explain your answer.

20 students' grades in a
Science test and a
French test

French test			
CREDIT	0	2	2
PASS	2	7	0
FAIL	5	1	1
	FAIL	PASS	CREDIT

Science test

12 For each of A, B, C and D sketch a possible
   scatter diagram.
   Under your diagrams write 'positive correlation',
   'negative correlation', or 'no correlation'.
   A: Shoe size and age for twenty 7 - 11 year olds.
   B: Shoe size and age for twenty 30 - 40 year olds.
   C: Mass and age for eighty 40 - 50 year old men.
   D: Mass and age for eighty 60 - 100 year old women.

Correlated letters
List 20 words of different
lengths:
2 with 1 letter
2 with 2 letters
2 with 3 letters
…
2 with 10 letters.
Does your list suggest any
correlation between the
number of letters in words
and the number of vowels
in words?
Explain how you decided.
•••••••••••••••••••••••••••••••

13 Name something which you think
   a) correlates positively with the number
      of cups of tea people drink in one week
   b) does not correlate with the number of
      cups of tea people drink in one week
   c) correlates negatively with the number of
      goals scored in a season by football teams.

14 Twenty five people take a driving test and a swimming test.
   The table shows the results.
   Pam says that there is no correlation between the results of
   the two tests.
   Do you think she is correct?
   Explain your answer.

Swimming test		
PASS	3	12
FAIL	2	8
	FAIL	PASS

Driving test

1   Pam turns over the three rectangular cards
    and five circular cards and shuffles them. ▶
    She chooses a rectangular card and then
    a circular card.
    One possible **outcome** is R2.

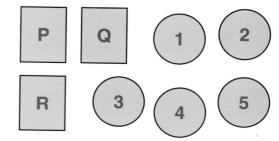

a) Write down another possible outcome.
b) Pam repeats the experiment.
   The rectangle card she chooses is Q.
   One possible outcome is now Q5.
   List all the possible outcomes.
c) List all the possible outcomes when
   her choice of circular card happens
   to be 4.
d) How many possible outcomes are
   there altogether for the experiment?

2   Alun has the four cards and the die.
    He turns the cards over and shuffles them.
    He chooses a card, then rolls the die.
    a) One possible outcome is W2.
       Write another possible outcome.
    b) Write all the possible outcomes when
       the card he chooses happens to be Y.
    c) How many possible outcomes are there
       for each choice of letter?
    d) How many possible outcomes are
       there altogether?
    e) Alun draws the chart. ▶
       Explain what you think it shows.
    f) Draw a similar chart for the
       experiment in Q1.

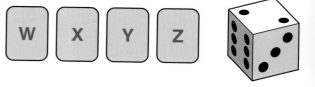

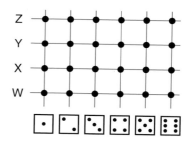

3   Mira has a Pink bead (P), a Yellow bead (Y) and a Green bead (G).
    She puts them in a bag.
    She also has an Orange fruit gum (O), a Lemon fruit gum (L),
    a Redcurrant fruit gum (R), and a Blackcurrant fruit gum (B).
    She puts them in a different bag.
    a) Mira takes out a bead and a fruitgum.
       One possible outcome is YL.
       Write another three possible outcomes.
    b) Draw a chart like that in Q2 to show all the possible outcomes.
    c) How many possible outcomes are there altogether?
    d) How many possible outcomes are there if Mira includes a
       Mango fruit gum?

4   Sandra spins the two spinners.
    a) One possible outcome is B2.
       List three more possible outcomes.
    b) List all the outcomes which begin C...
    c) Sandra begins to draw diagram X
       to show all the possible outcomes.
       Copy and complete it.
    d) Diagram Y gives another way of
       showing all the outcomes.
       Copy and complete it.

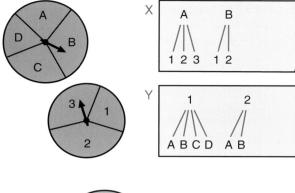

5   Hanif spins these two spinners.
    a) One possible outcome is Q2.
       List three more possible outcomes.
    b) Draw a diagram like one of those in Q4
       to show all of the outcomes.
    c) How many possible outcomes are there?
    d) How many outcomes would there be if
       the first spinner had 3 different regions,
       P, Q and R ?

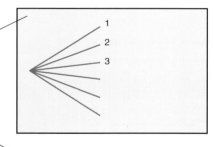

6   a) Marcia has a die and a coin.
       She starts to draw a diagram to show
       the possible outcomes for the die.
       Copy and complete it.
    b) Marcia thinks of throwing the die
       and spinning the coin.
       She extends her diagram to include
       the possible outcomes for the coin.
       For example, a 1 on the die can be
       followed by a Tail or a Head on the
       coin.
       Extend the diagram you drew in
       part a) to include all the outcomes
       for the coin.
    c) Copy and complete the list of possible
       outcomes for throwing the die and
       spinning the coin. ▶

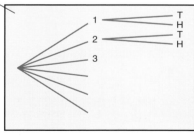

Possible
outcomes

1T

1H

2T

2H

7   The diagram you drew in part b) of Q 6
    is called a **tree diagram**. It shows all the
    possible outcomes for the experiment.

    This is another version which can be drawn
    for throwing the die and spinning the coin. ▶
    Copy and complete it.

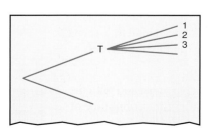

8   Jim spins the coin and the spinner together.
    He begins to draw this tree diagram. ▶
    a) Copy and complete Jim's diagram.
    b) Draw an alternative tree diagram which shows all the possible outcomes.

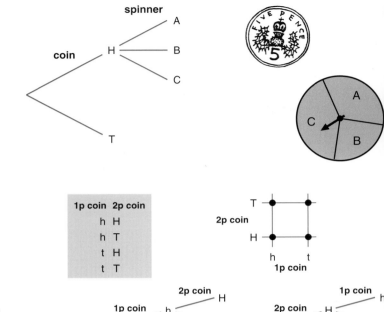

9   These are four different ways of showing all the possible outcomes when two coins (a 1p and a 2p) are spun together.
    Find four different ways of showing all the possible outcomes when one of three coloured beads (red, green and blue) is taken from a bag, and a coin is spun.

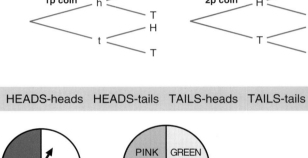

10 The list shows the four possible outcomes for spinning two coins. Each outcome is equally likely, so the probability of each is $\frac{1}{4}$.
    a) List the possible outcomes for spinning the two spinners.
    b) What is the probability for each outcome?

HEADS-heads   HEADS-tails   TAILS-heads   TAILS-tails

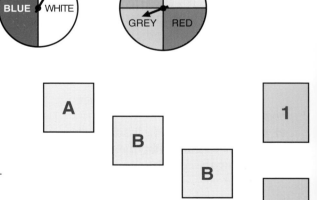

11 Francesco chooses a square card and a rectangular card.
    He says:
    X: There are four possible outcomes, A1, B1, A2 and B2.
    Y: The probability of each outcome is $\frac{1}{4}$.
    a) Is his statement X correct? Explain your answer.
    b) Is his statement Y correct? Explain your answer.

    A   B   B   1   2

12 You spin a coin and roll a die. What is the probability of scoring Heads-6 ?

1   Look at the spinner.
    The probabilty of scoring A is $\frac{1}{4}$.
    a) What is the probability of scoring B ?
    b) Add the probabilities for A and B.
        Write down the result.

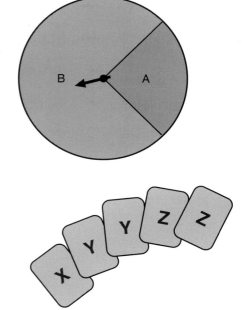

> The only possible outcomes for the spinner are
> A and B.
> So it is certain that we will get A *or* B.
> So the probabilities for A and B must add up to 1.

2   Jim turns over the five cards, shuffles them and
    chooses one.
    a) Write down the probability that he chooses
        (i) an X   (ii) a Y   (iii) a Z.
    b) Add the probabilities for the three outcomes,
        X, Y and Z.
    c) Is your result in part b) as you would expect?
        Explain your answer.

3   The probabilities for all the possible outcomes of an event must add up
    to 1, because it is certain that one of the outcomes will occur.

    a) What is the probability that
        A: it will either rain or not rain in your home town tomorrow
        B: tomorrow you will either see a pigeon or you will not see a pigeon
        C: in their next game, Manchester United will win, or draw, or lose,
            or the game will be abandoned
        D: when you throw a die you will score 1 or a number larger than 1 ?
    b) Write down an example of your own like those in part a).

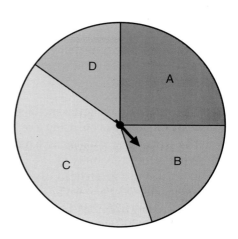

4   Look at the spinner.
    a) The probability that you will score A is $\frac{1}{4}$.
        What is the probability that you will not score A ?
    b) The probability that you will score B is $\frac{1}{5}$.
        What is the probability that you will not score B ?
    c) The probability that you will score C is $\frac{2}{5}$.
        What is the probability that you will not score C ?
    d) What fraction of the spinner is taken up altogether
        by the B and C sectors?
    e) What is the probability that you will score B or C
        on the spinner?
    f) What is the probability that you will score neither
        B nor C ?

5   A bag of mixed nuts contains peanuts,
cob nuts and cashew nuts.
A nut falls out of the bag.
The probability that it is a peanut is $\frac{4}{7}$.
The probability that it is a cob nut is $\frac{2}{7}$.
What is the probability that it is
a) *not* a peanut
b) *not* a cob nut
c) *either* a peanut *or* a cob nut
d) a cashew nut?

6   Des buys a lottery ticket.
The probability that he will win the jackpot is 1 in 14 million.
a) Write this probability as a fraction.
b) Write the probability that Des will not win as a fraction.

7   a) The probability that it will rain tomorrow is 0.7.
What is the probability that it will not rain?
b) What is the probability of scoring 5 on a die?
c) What is the probability of not scoring 5 on a die?
d) The probability that a bank will be robbed in
Atlantic City tomorrow is 0.09.
What is the probability that a bank will not be
robbed in Atlantic City tomorrow?

8   Malik's birthday is on 3rd July.
The weather records for his home town suggest a probability
of 0.35 that it will rain on his next birthday.
Jo says 'The probability that the sun will shine must be 0.65'.
Is Jo correct? Explain why.

9   Usha throws a plastic flower pot into the air.
She records how often it lands on its base: 19 times in 100 trials.
Usha says: The probability that it lands upside down is $\frac{81}{100}$.
Is she correct? Explain why.

10 There are some red, green and blue beads in a bag.
The probability of choosing a red bead is 0.24.
The probability of choosing a blue bead is 0.54.
What is the probability of
a) choosing a green bead
b) not choosing a green bead
c) choosing a red bead or a blue bead
d) choosing a green bead or a blue bead?